TRANSFIGURATION

JOHN DEAR

TRANSFIGURATION

A

MEDITATION

ON

TRANSFORMING OURSELVES

AND

OUR WORLD

IMAGE BOOKS

Doubleday

New York London Toronto Sydney Auckland

AN IMAGE BOOK
PUBLISHED BY DOUBLEDAY

Published in the United States by Doubleday, an imprint of
The Doubleday Broadway Publishing Group, a division of
Random House, Inc., New York.
www.doubleday.com

IMAGE, DOUBLEDAY, and the portrayal of a deer drinking from a
stream are registered trademarks of Random House, Inc.

Book design by Michael Collica

Library of Congress Cataloging-in-Publication Data
Dear, John, 1959–
Transfiguration : a meditation on transforming ourselves and our
world / John Dear.–1st ed.
p. cm.
1. Christian life. 2. Spiritual life–Christianity.
BV4501.3 .D445 2006
248.4–dc22   2006013667

ISBN 978-0-385-51008-0

PRINTED IN THE UNITED STATES OF AMERICA

1 3 5 7 9 10 8 6 4 2

First Edition

For Joe Markwordt

Jesus took Peter, John, and James and went up the mountain to pray. While he was praying his face changed in appearance and his clothing became dazzling white. And behold, two men were conversing with him, Moses and Elijah, who appeared in glory and spoke of his exodus that he was going to accomplish in Jerusalem. Peter and his companions had been overcome by sleep, but becoming fully awake, they saw his glory and the two men standing with him. As they were about to part from him, Peter said to Jesus, "Master, it is good that we are here; let us make three tents, one for you, one for Moses, and one for Elijah." But he did not know what he was saying. While he was still speaking, a cloud came and cast a shadow over them, and they became frightened when they entered the cloud. Then from the cloud came a voice that said, "This is my chosen Son; listen to him." After the voice had spoken, Jesus was found alone. They fell silent and did not at that time tell anyone what they had seen.

–LUKE 9:28-36

When we told you about the power and coming of our Lord Jesus Christ, we were not slavishly repeating cleverly intended myths. No, we had seen his majesty with our own eyes . . . when we were with him on the holy mountain.

–2 PETER 1:16-18

This is the meaning of the transfiguration for Jesus himself: in the dark night of hopelessness, the light of God shines and a human heart finds in God the power which turns a dying into victory and redemption for the world.

−Karl Rahner

The theology of transfiguration is saying that the road of redemption passes through the cross and through Calvary, but that the goal of Christians is beyond history, not to alienate oneself from history but rather to give more meaning to history, a definitive meaning. From the day of Christ's resurrection there remained burning in the same history of time a torch of eternity.

−Oscar Romero

Maybe we do not always fully recognize our mountaintop experiences. We write them off as insignificant and trivial compared with all the important and urgent things we have to do. Still, Jesus wants us to see his glory, so that we can cling to that experience in moments of doubt, despair, or anguish. When we are attentive to the light within us and around us, we will gradually see more and more of that light and even become a light for others. We have to trust that the transfiguration experience is closer to us than we might think.

−Henri Nouwen

CONTENTS

Contents

_____

by Archbishop Desmond Tutu

Quite often during the difficult days of our struggle against the viciousness of apartheid's injustice, I would say that much of our involvement was in fact exhilarating. I must have sounded strange, as if somehow we were masochists. But the exhilaration stemmed from the fact that we had on hand a remarkable instrument, the Bible. It was really as if it had been compiled with our particular circumstances in view. It was such a thoroughly revolutionary tool that we frequently would say, "If you intend to oppress people, then don't hand them the Bible, for nothing is more subversive of injustice and oppression than the Bible."

Those who hoped that oppressed people would remain docile and would kowtow were in for a rude shock. They contended that what invested people with worth was something extrinsic, really a biological irrelevance–skin color or ethnicity. By definition it could not be a universal phenomenon but something possessed by some, who belonged to the thus privileged elite. The Bible exploded that myth because the Bible proclaimed that our worth as human beings was intrinsic, it belonged in the definition of what constituted a human being. It was possessed by all without exception, and it was that each one of us was created in the image of God. And so we would say to our people, "When they despise you and treat you as a nonentity, hold your head high, because you are God's representative, you are God's viceroy. You are a God-carrier, or as St. Paul declared, 'We are each a sanctuary, a temple, of the Holy Spirit.' " This knowledge would eventually come to bear on the ghastly machinations of apartheid.

For those who pietistically claimed that God treated us even-handedly because, as they wanted to claim, God was neutral, we had many biblical texts to refer to which showed that God was in fact notoriously biased. Try telling Pharaoh after his showdown with Moses and the catastrophe, from the Egyptian point of view, of the Exodus, that God was neutral. In what was to be the paradigmatic event par excellence of the Bible, God sided with an obstreperous rabble of slaves against one of the leading monarchs of the day. This divine bias was demonstrated no more dramatically than in the story of Naboth's vineyard in 1 Kings. Naboth, in the story, does not even rate a genealogy; thus, in the convention of the day, he was a real nobody. Kings in those days could do almost anything they liked. Well, yes, everywhere, but not in Israel. Elijah intervened in the name of Israel's God on behalf of this so-called nonentity.

For us in South Africa, where the apartheid government uprooted people from their ancestral homes to dump them in poverty-stricken Bantustan homelands, this story was like manna from heaven. It spoke of a God who cared. We used to say that, yes, this God was the same yesterday, today, and forever—that just as God operated during the Exodus, so God would operate in our case too. For this God was not deaf but heard their cries of anguish because of apartheid's oppression. God was not blind, was not stupid, and God would come down to deliver them as God had done so long ago. This God did not give useful advice from a safe distance but entered the fiery furnace to be there with God's servants because this God was Immanuel, "God with us."

If you were in this God's community, God's people, then you had to reflect God's character, to "be holy for I am holy" (Leviticus 19:2)—but not with a holiness defined by ritual purity. No, it was a holiness that was dynamic, revealed in how you treated the poor—in, for instance, not picking all the harvest but leaving something deliberately behind for those who appeared more and more to be God's favorites—the poor, the widow, the orphan, and the alien, who in most societies tended to be those with the least clout. If you were king over this God's people and you were given God's righteousness to rule as God's representative, this was shown by your special care for the poor, the weak, the downtrodden (as in Psalm 72).

The prophet must have shocked his contemporaries when in God's name he declared their religious observances to be obnoxious, an unacceptable abomination, as Isaiah did (see Isaiah 1), saying their religious acts were acceptable only if they issued in a concern for the widow, the orphan, and the alien. God rejected even the most meticulously observed fast as unacceptable, declaring, to the chagrin of the worshipers, that the genuine fast was setting the captive free, clothing the naked, and feeding the hungry (Isaiah 58), to be echoed much later in Our Lord's parable of the Last Judgment (Matthew 25). To be anointed by the Spirit of this God was to be inspired to do not conventionally churchy or pious things but thoroughly mundane, political things—setting free the imprisoned, loosing the bonds of the enslaved, preaching good news, especially to the poor (not exclusively materially poor, of course), and announcing the Jubilee Year of the Lord, with its implications of releasing people from mortgages and debts and trying to produce a utopia where people could have their land back (Isaiah 61).

There were in South Africa the usual cries about the awfulness of preachers of the Gospel mixing religion with politics, and we asked what Bible those accusers were reading. It was almost always those who were beneficiaries of a particular oppressive status quo who complained about the heinous crime of using pulpits for political ends. We used to retort that the poor, the hungry, the oppressed hardly ever made this charge. If anything, they might have complained that we were not sufficiently political. What could have been more political than a God who helped a rabble of slaves to escape or a prophet preaching that his compatriots should cross over to the enemy besieging their capital city? What price patriotism? We used to have to ask, If God's writ did not run in the political realm, whose did?

And so we were able to declare to our people that those who sought to uphold an unjust dispensation had in fact already lost the fight, no matter how formidable and fearsome their arsenal. God was in charge in this moral universe. There was no way in which injustice, oppression, wrong, and evil would have the last word. The perpetrators of evil would bite the dust as surely as night followed day. St. Paul's assertion "If God be for us, who can be against us?" was our watchword.

I have sensed a like exhilaration, a thrill, in John Dear's splendid disquisition on the Transfiguration. Traditionally, the account of Our Lord's transfiguration and its sequel in the healing of the boy possessed by a demon has been interpreted as providing a paradigm of the encounter with God leading to engagement with the world, with evil, that the spiritual experience is not meant to insulate us against the rigors of life as experienced by most of God's children in a hostile world out there.

This is the first time I have come across an exegesis that so compellingly and persuasively argues that the chief end of such a deeply spiritual experience, the encounter with God on God's mountain, prepares the one who undergoes it for confrontation with the forces of evil even unto death for the sake of God's shalom, that we who in different ways have transfiguration moments should all be stalwarts for that peace. It is not an optional extra. The encounter with God would constrain us to work for a new ordering of society, where we would beat our swords into plowshares and our spears into pruning hooks and we would study war no more (as both Isaiah and Micah declare in identical words). It is to see a fulfillment of God's dream, a new heaven and a new earth, when God will wipe away all tears and the wolf and the lamb will feed together and the lion will eat straw like the ox–"For they shall not hurt or destroy on all my holy mountain, says the Lord" (Isaiah 65:25).

This book is a clarion call for us to be engaged in the project for world peace. We ignore it at our peril.

–Cape Town, South Africa
January 2006

TRANSFIGURATION

INTRODUCTION

W hen I first met the great Jesuit peacemaker and poet Father Daniel Berrigan, I wanted his advice about the life that lay ahead for me, but I didn't know exactly what to say. "What's the point of all this?" I finally asked him.

Dan took my awkward question seriously. "All we have to do is make our lives fit into the story of Jesus," he said. "We have to get our lives to make sense in light of the Gospel."

What a helpful answer! I never forgot it. The Christian life, I was learning, is fashioned after the life of Jesus. As his followers, we have to know his story, enter his story, and make our story part of his story. The Gospel, in other words, is the measure of our lives.

According to the story, after several years of nonstop service, preaching, healing, and other public works, Jesus retreated up a mountain in search of prayerful solitude, the affirming presence of his beloved God, and the strength to go forward to the cross. His spiritual experience on the mountaintop confirmed his public mission to seek justice, make peace, and lay down his life for humanity. This contemplative event renewed his determination to go to Jerusalem no matter what, because it was there, on the mountain, that God again called him "my beloved." It was there on the mountain that his self-understanding was confirmed in person by Moses and Elijah, who encouraged him to fulfill his vocation as the nonviolent Messiah. It was there on the mountain that he experienced a foretaste of the glory to come in God's reign of light and resurrection.

By sharing that experience with his friends, Jesus passed on a great lesson. We too can take time from our life journey, climb the mountain of God, and recognize the risen Christ in our midst. We too can awake to see the transfigured Christ before us and hear the voice of God instruct us to listen more attentively to Jesus and do what he says. We too can take heart and go forward into the world with the Gospel mission of serving the needy, resisting evil, doing good, and proclaiming peace. We too can receive a glimpse of the new life to come in God's reign of light and resurrection.

Every one of us can have a transfiguration experience at some point in our lives if we dare follow Jesus all the way to the cross and resurrection. The more we enter into the story of Jesus, the more we too will share his every experience. At some point, we too will have a sacramental experience of hearing God call us God's beloved, as Jesus did when he sat by the Jordan River after his baptism. We too can share his public ministry of healing, teaching, challenging injustice, and promoting justice. We too can enter his private life of community with friends, table fellowship with the marginalized, and intimate solitude with God. At some point, as we walk the road to our own Jerusalems, we too can climb the mountain of God and suddenly recognize Christ in our midst. We too can hear God tell us once again to listen to him.

If we dare listen to Jesus and follow him closely on the road to peace, I am learning, we too are transformed, and at some point, if only for a moment, even transfigured. Our lives are changed into light and love, we realize that we are God's beloved sons and daughters, and we shed Christ's light for others, guiding them through this world of darkness. We ourselves glimpse the new life of resurrection to come. Encouraged by the transfigured Christ, by our own modern-day Moseses and Elijahs, we take another step on the Gospel journey of nonviolence into the world's violence. We listen closely to the words of Jesus and put them into practice. We even find strength to carry the cross of nonviolent resistance to injustice and welcome the risen Christ's gift of peace in our hearts and in the world.

By walking with Jesus and sharing in his work here and now, we meet the transfigured Christ, who, in turn, transforms us, confirms our mission, and encourages us to continue his work for the reign of God. If we remain faithful to the journey, we will be transfigured, persecuted, crucified, and risen—and the risen Christ himself will welcome us home into the house of light and peace.

This little meditation on the story of Jesus' transfiguration grows out of my own discipleship journey over these last difficult years for the Church and the world. As I meditate on my journey and the story of the Transfiguration, I discover again that all we have to do is walk with Jesus, listen to Jesus, wait for Jesus, love Jesus, be with Jesus, serve Jesus, see Jesus in suffering humanity, practice Jesus' way of active nonviolence, and welcome Jesus' reign of peace.

The best way to understand life in these tumultuous times, then, is to see it as a pilgrimage journey on the road with Jesus. I am learning once again that, as we enter into the story of Jesus and continue his mission of love and peace, we will see the living Christ transfigured in our midst. We will hear the voice of God call us to listen and be reenergized to go forward on the Gospel journey. Though we will undoubtedly face the cross, if we heed the transfigured Christ and follow him step by step down the mountain to Jerusalem, ready to proclaim the good news of peace and practice his compassionate love, somehow, some way, someday, we too will share his resurrection. The transfiguration is the sign of that promise.

I have broken this little meditation into five parts–walking in the footsteps of Jesus; going up the mountain with Jesus; recognizing the transfigured Christ in our midst; going down the mountain to the cross; and fulfilling our mission of transfiguration nonviolence in a culture of violence and war. Each part begins with a few basic suggestions or guideposts for our steps along the transfiguration journey. Each part concludes with a few questions for your personal reflection and prayer.

May this little book encourage you on your discipleship journey into the story of Jesus. May you be blessed as you journey up the mountain to meet the transfigured Jesus and follow him down the mountain as his disciple into the world of war, injustice, and violence on the Gospel mission of peace, love, and nonviolence.

John Dear
Madrid, New Mexico

PART ONE

LIFE IN THE FOOTSTEPS OF JESUS

Steps Along the Transfiguration Journey

1. Try to live your life more and more every day in relationship with Jesus.

2. Take a few minutes of quality, quiet time in contemplative prayer every day to sit with Jesus, talk with him, and listen to him. Share your pain, problems, and hopes with Jesus.

3. Begin to see and know Jesus as a faithful friend, compassionate companion, and beloved Lord.

4. Take a few minutes every day to read a few verses from one of the four Gospels so that you become more and more familiar with the life story of Jesus.

5. Reflect on your life journey and notice when and where you were walking with Jesus, and what keeps you from Jesus.

6. See how your life fits into Jesus' life story right now.

7. Choose to enter more and more into the life journey of Jesus, and try to walk every day from now on in his footsteps.

8. Try to walk beside Jesus, with Jesus, every day for the rest of your life journey.

1.

On the Road with Jesus

In the summer of 1982, when I was twenty-one, I walked alone through Israel from Jerusalem to Bethlehem to Nazareth to Galilee on a pilgrimage to see for myself the land that Jesus knew. I had spent the previous year working odd jobs in Washington, D.C., saving up for the trip as one last voyage into the world before I entered the Jesuits. It was the middle of June when I boarded an Amtrak train to New York City's Penn Station, walked to Thirty-first Street, and said a prayer in St. Francis of Assisi Church. Then I caught a cab to JFK Airport.

Unfortunately, just then, Israel invaded Lebanon. Many people canceled their plane tickets. I decided to go ahead with my adventure. Instead of the quiet pilgrimage I had envisioned, however, I found myself in a war zone. As I stepped off the plane that day in Tel Aviv, I was greeted with machine guns and interrogated. Wherever I went during those weeks, I saw not the dream of faith, hope, and love but the nightmare of bombs, tanks, and jets. My life would never be the same.

Toward the end of that summer pilgrimage, on a hot July morning, I rode the local Galilee bus from the sea town of Tiberias some twenty miles to the foot of Mount Tabor, the large, round mountain where tradition holds that Jesus was transfigured before his disciples, where Moses and Elijah appeared to him and God spoke from the clouds. After the bus driver let me off and drove on down the deserted road, I stood alone at the foot of the mountain, looking up. I still remember my excitement as I started up the dirt path, through the bushes and olive trees to the mountaintop, thinking about the mystery of the Transfiguration, thrilled and trembling to be climbing the mountain of God.

According to the Gospels, the Transfiguration marks one of the few overtly mystical experiences in Jesus' life. He was on his way to Jerusalem, where he would engage in nonviolent civil disobedience in the Temple, an act that would lead the authorities to arrest and execute him. On the mountain, in that place of solitude and beauty, God transformed him and gave him a taste of the resurrected life to come. He became the Christ he would become. Suddenly, Jesus' three closest friends realized that their rabbi was much more than a wise teacher or radical revolutionary. They knew, in fact, that he was the Holy One of God.

Whether the event actually occurred after the resurrection, as some Scripture scholars suggest, or whether it is meant to place Jesus as the fulfillment of the tradition of Moses and Elijah, representatives of the law and the prophets, something dramatic happened to Jesus on that mountaintop, and he found the strength to go back down to resist the empire and fulfill his destiny as the Suffering Servant.

It was blistering hot under a clear blue sky the day I climbed Mount Tabor. I carried only my backpack, with a few clothes, a camera, and a Bible. The road zigzagged, slowly making its way through trees and rocks to the top. The arduous climb often left me exhausted, but I was strangely exhilarated, overwhelmed to walk in the steps of Jesus, to see the land he saw. I rested under the olive trees and marveled at the panoramic view. I looked out at the beautiful brown hills and uninhabited valleys that spread as far as I could see.

After several hours of climbing, I reached the top. I continued along the path toward the majestic towers of the basilica, the huge Church of the Transfiguration, the sole building on the mountain, which commemorates the great event.

I approached the massive church with awe and wonder, walking slowly, mindfully, one step at a time. As I came near the structure, I saw that the front doors stood wide open. Taking a deep breath, I stepped inside, gazed at the huge mosaic of the Transfiguration, and realized there was no one else in sight. I was alone on the mountaintop.

I sat in a pew and beheld the bright, colorful mosaics depicting Jesus in his white robes talking to the biblical prophets while the three disciples slept on the ground. After offering a prayer for my life, my family, and the world, I walked outside, sat down, and looked out at the magnificent view of the hills, mountains, valleys, and in the distance, the Sea of Galilee.

If Jesus ever wanted to get away from the crowds, to be alone with a few friends, to pray and reflect on his difficult journey to Jerusalem, this surely was the place. From that mountaintop, I gained a bird's-eye view and saw the world as if from God's vantage point. As I took a deep breath and looked up at the sky, my heart beat fast. I was grateful to be alive. This was—literally and figuratively—a peak experience.

In the peace of that mountaintop moment, I felt loved by the Creator of the world and experienced new hope for myself and humanity. Not only was I not alone but I was deeply loved by God. Like the disciples in the story, I was waking up to reality. I perceived an invitation to walk with Jesus down the mountain to Jerusalem, into the heart of the world, where he would risk everything for love of the whole human race, and where I might dare that same risky, all-inclusive, sacrificial love.

From that mountaintop, the journey into the heart of the world, to Jerusalem, made eminent sense. I could see the road ahead, the inevitable tragic outcome, the world's repeated rejection of God's gift of peace. I also could see the glorious epilogue, God's resurrection of Christ and the crucified peoples of history, and the risen Christ's gift of peace. I felt renewed in spirit. Yes, I could go forward in faith and hope to walk the discipleship journey with the Holy One of God.

I started down the mountain, brimming with hope, praising God, bursting with love for everyone, ready to take on the world, to uproot mountains, end wars, convert the masses, heal the sick, and raise the dead. I felt so high because I knew that I was walking with Jesus, and that he would do these things. All the way down I sang an Easter hymn of resurrection. The chorus was easy: "Alleluia! Alleluia! Alleluia!"

Whenever I get the chance to speak with others about the spiritual life, I share this basic truth, that we are on a journey with God through life toward death and new life. If we choose, we can transform our life journey immeasurably by deliberately following in the footsteps of Jesus. Through contemplative prayer, Gospel study, and shared community, we can learn to walk with him and let him lead us where he will. Even though we fall flat on our faces time and time again, he always helps us up and enables us to take another step forward on the journey home to God's house of love and peace.

If we can respond to this call and try to follow Jesus, our lives will be transfigured because they are no longer our own. They will belong to Jesus. They take on universal meaning and find a place in the cosmic scheme of creation.

But we cannot find that place on our own. If we hand over our lives to Jesus and start walking with him, he will lead us to new places, new people, and new truths, so that the journey is no longer a journey from crisis to crisis, from death to death, but from life to new life, peace to deeper peace, glory to even greater glory. As we walk with Jesus, we find ourselves entering his story and beginning to share his life. Like Jesus, we start serving the poor, healing the broken, liberating the oppressed, speaking up for justice, and making peace. All kinds of miracles occur, not by any effort of our own but by the grace of God working through our brokenness and discipleship. Our lives suddenly blossom. We come alive because our lives are now in the service of the God of life.

For the Christian, life makes most sense as a journey in the footsteps of Jesus. With Jesus, there is not only purpose, meaning, and direction but unconditional love, unlimited compassion, unbounded forgiveness, real hope, and true peace. With Jesus, we have the love of God present and available to us, guiding us through life, showing us how to live, teaching us to serve one another, giving us a mission on behalf of humanity, and leading us home into the fullness of peace.

I can think of no greater life than radical discipleship to Jesus. Companionship and friendship with Jesus, and the Gospel works of justice and peace that this life entails, may sound quaint, pious, and naïve, if not idealistic or surreal, but I submit, as the saints and martyrs testified, that it is the most authentic and rewarding life. Each one of us can choose to live our days in the company of Jesus, to walk in his footsteps, enter his story, and become his friend and companion.

If we dare undertake the discipleship journey and remain faithful to Jesus, one day we will look back on our lives and realize that we were never alone, that our lives have borne good fruit, and that we have fulfilled the mission God intended for us. On that day, Jesus will welcome us home as his best friends and companions. At that moment, we will rejoice at the immense gift given to us, the blessings we have received, and the warm welcome we have been offered. The journey will end because we have fully entered into the presence of Jesus to dwell in his company in peace and joy forever. That moment makes every step of the discipleship journey worth the price.

2.

Living in Relationship with Jesus

Before Mother Teresa founded the Missionaries of Charity, she spent twenty years teaching secluded, well-to-do high school girls as a Sister of Loreto in India. Then one day, while riding the train to Darjeeling to make her annual retreat, in a moment of "intimate prayer with Jesus," as she later described it, she heard a voice tell her to leave the order and serve "the poorest of the poor." She obeyed, and for the rest of her life she lived with that intimate prayer, served the poorest of the poor, and walked with Jesus. As all the world knows, she helped tens of thousands of dying people, missioned thousands more into the life of loving discipleship, and inspired millions around the globe.

Martin Sheen tells the story of visiting Mother Teresa in San Diego in the early 1990s, along with a popular motivational speaker. This speaker was in great demand, appearing frequently on television, addressing conventions and business conferences, telling people how they could become successful. He is a tall, outgoing man, and he towered over the diminutive Mother Teresa when they met.

"How did you manage to become so successful, so famous?" he asked Mother Teresa.

She looked up at him, smiled, and said confidently, "Jesus."

"No, I mean, how is that you run such a huge religious institution, serve the most desperate people, travel constantly, and yet touch so many people?" he continued.

"Jesus," she said again, with a big smile.

"No, I'm asking how you do it," he persisted, still not satisfied. "How do you continue to live this life, speak to millions, win the respect of the world, and manage to be one of the greatest people in the world, even in the history of the world?"

"Jesus," Mother Teresa answered once again with a beaming smile.

The man shook his head and turned away, totally mystified. He had no idea what she was talking about.

Martin Sheen was delighted and amazed by the exchange and her childlike yet powerful answer. He thought Mother Teresa was brilliant, compelling, and entirely convincing through her simplicity and transparency, and he was stunned by her reliance on the person of Jesus.

Reliance on Jesus is the heart of the Christian life. The saints testify that the key to their lives was not their great accomplishments, their terrible sufferings, their bold prophecies, or even their astonishing miracles. It was Jesus. Somehow, he had touched them, invited them to follow him, and managed to walk by their side. Through his grace, they remained faithful to him, rooting everything they did in their intimate relationship with him. Their lives made sense and bore good fruit because they were centered on Jesus.

All the outstanding figures of the past century exemplify this devotion to Jesus. Dorothy Day, founder of the Catholic Worker, wrote shortly before her death in 1980 that she was grateful and lucky because "Jesus has been on my mind nearly every day of my life."

Standing alone on the balcony of the Lorraine Motel in Memphis, Tennessee, at 5:50 P.M. on April 4, 1968, Martin Luther King, Jr., called down to the gospel singer Ben Branch in the parking lot below and told him to sing King's favorite hymn at the rally that evening. Just as he named the words of the hymn, "Precious Lord, take my hand," King was shot through the throat and killed.

On his way to a special evening Mass where he was assassinated on Monday, March 24, 1980, the Salvadoran archbishop Oscar Romero stopped at the Jesuit community house in Santa Tecla, a suburb of San Salvador, to receive the sacrament of reconciliation. He told his Jesuit confessor, "I want to appear clean before the Lord."

The Hindu peacemaker Mahatma Gandhi lived in a bare mud hut in his ashram in Wardha, with only one picture on the wall: a small portrait of Jesus walking on a road, with a caption that read, "He is our peace."

Flannery O'Connor began her classic novel *Wise Blood* with the observation that integrity for her meant not being able to get rid of the "Ragged Figure moving from tree to tree in the back of the mind."

We see reliance on Jesus in the last words of the Trappist monk and spiritual writer Thomas Merton in Bangkok on

December 10, 1968, when he had just finished his lecture "Marxism and Monasticism." Many of the abbots, prioresses, and other monks present were disturbed by the talk because it was not what they expected; they did not agree with his broad vision of modern religious life. As Merton walked to his room to take an afternoon nap, one of the monks approached him and told him that a nun in the audience had been disappointed because he had said nothing about evangelization. "What we are asked to do at present," Merton said to the monk, "is not so much to speak of Christ as to let him live in us so that people may find him by feeling how he lives in us."

In 1993, while sharing a prison cell with the antinuclear activist Philip Berrigan, who died in 2002, I discovered a piece of paper listing all the biblical names for Jesus, such as Son of God, Son of Humanity, Lamb of God, Root of Jesse, Prince of Peace, Good Shepherd, and Bread of Life. I asked Phil about it, and he explained that he was memorizing this list so he could recite the names as a mantra and call upon Jesus throughout the day to help him, sustain him, and strengthen him.

These modern-day saints shared an intimate knowledge of Jesus and lived in daily relationship with him. They thought about him, sought after him, and talked about him. They fashioned their lives after him and walked in his footsteps. Others turned to them because they felt the presence of Jesus in these people's lives, words, and deeds. They urged everyone to do the same. Live in relationship with Jesus, they said, and your life will be transformed and you will begin to do God's will.

Whenever I lead a retreat, I ask the participants to reflect on the presence of Jesus in their lives. "When did Jesus call you? When have you felt the presence of Jesus? Where do you feel Jesus in your life now? What is your experience of Jesus? Who is Jesus for you? What do you find attractive about the life of Jesus? Where do you see Jesus in the world? Where is he leading you? What would it look like for you to become his friend and companion? How can you deepen your relationship with Jesus? What does discipleship to Jesus mean for you?" Such questions can help open up the spiritual life and encourage us on our journey toward becoming modern-day saints and apostles, friends of Jesus.

As I read the lives of saints, I notice that, as they grew older, they wanted simply to be with Jesus and do God's will. Likewise, the older we get, the more dissatisfied we are with our selfish pursuits. We will want more and more to be with Jesus, to know Jesus, to love Jesus, to listen to Jesus, to follow Jesus, and to do exactly what Jesus wants. With him, we feel centered, happier, and at peace. Anything can happen because Jesus walks with us. Even better, miracles will transform us and the whole world if we dare walk with him.

3.

_____

The Measure of the Gospel

To live according to the Gospel of Jesus, we need to ponder his story and make choices so that our life journey begins to resemble his. Before we reflect on his transfiguration for clues about our journey up the mountain, it may be helpful to look at the events that led him to the mountain.

According to Luke's Gospel, from the moment Jesus was baptized and emerged from his fast in the desert until the day he climbed Mount Tabor, he astonished everyone with dazzling words and miraculous deeds. He walked many miles, taught enormous crowds, healed the sick, expelled demons, and raised the dead. He was utterly amazing.

His few years of public activity were packed with one spectacular event after another. In nearly every episode, Jesus challenged the imperial and religious authorities who oppressed and killed the poor. Time and time again, he broke the law by consorting with the unclean, violating the Sabbath, proclaiming himself a king, urging people not to pay taxes, and disrupting the banking transactions in the Temple sanctuary. Jesus was bold, daring, and provocative. He was perfectly nonviolent but never passive.

Jesus was determined not to play God, but to be as human, as real, as possible. In a world where everyone wants to be God, it is precisely this daring humanity that got him in trouble. It is not surprising then that, in the midst of his whirlwind activity, he led three friends up a sacred mountain for quiet contemplative prayer before continuing his revolutionary mission.

As I review the events that led Jesus to Mount Tabor, I see him engaging in three general activities: announcing God's reign of peace and justice while at the same time denouncing injustice; teaching the wisdom of creative nonviolence; and serving, healing, and liberating the poor and oppressed.

Announcing God's Reign of Peace and Justice

According to the Gospel of Luke, after walking through the Galilean countryside proclaiming God's reign, Jesus returned home to Nazareth, where he entered the synagogue, opened the Scriptures to the Book of Isaiah, and read aloud God's mandate to make justice a reality for the poor here and now:

The Spirit of the Lord is upon me, because he has
anointed me to bring good news to the poor. He has
sent me to proclaim liberty to prisoners, and recovery of
sight to the blind, to let the oppressed go free, and to
proclaim the Jubilee year. (Luke 4:18–19)

When he finished, everyone looked intently at him. "Today this scripture passage is fulfilled in your hearing," he said. The congregation was stunned! They could not believe their ears. But after their initial fascination, they turned on him. Like the prophets of old, he began to criticize their social injustice and their complicity with imperial violence. He said that the holy prophets were never sent to them during their time of need because they were violent and unjust, and instead, the prophets were sent into enemy territory, where they healed the sick. God had blessed their enemies, not them, because they, the chosen ones, had been unfaithful and unjust.

The townspeople were outraged. They ran Jesus out of the synagogue to the brink of a nearby cliff, where they intended to throw him off. He barely escaped with his life.

Such an episode would shake any of us to the core, yet this public catastrophe in his hometown was just the first of a long series of heated exchanges, personal attacks, death threats, and assassination attempts against Jesus.

That first explosion in the Nazareth synagogue was certainly important for Jesus because, according to Luke, he had deliberately searched the Scriptures for a passage that summed up his life mission. Jesus was truly filled with the Spirit of the Lord. He was determined to bring good news to the poor, liberty to prisoners, vision to the blind, freedom to the oppressed, and the jubilee year of Leviticus, when all property and possessions would be redistributed equally among all people, regardless of class, race, religion, or nationality.

But he could have chosen a different passage. For example, he could have picked a text proclaiming God's greatness or condemning God's enemies. He could have picked a more explicitly prayerful, spiritual, or mystical verse. Instead, he chose a text with a political, revolutionary vision, thus aligning himself with the prophets, in particular the nonviolent rebel Isaiah. Jesus would dedicate his life to justice for the poor, the imprisoned, the blind, the oppressed, and the homeless. He became an activist, a troublemaker, a rabble-rouser, and a revolutionary. He embarked on a dangerous, political journey for the disarmament and transformation of the whole world.

Jesus was incapable of remaining silent in the face of social injustice, infidelity, violence, and idolatry, and so he caused trouble everywhere he went. Whenever anyone speaks out against one's culture, there is a backlash. People explode with rage. If we are going to follow Jesus on his journey, we too must speak up, announce God's reign of peace and justice, denounce war and injustice, and brace ourselves for a hostile reaction. We too must face the rejection of those around us, beginning with our hometown families and friends.

This first episode in Jesus' public life haunts me. As I crisscross the nation giving lectures to tens of thousands of people every year, speaking out against war and nuclear weapons and discussing the benefits of disarmament and justice, I have faced a variety of crowds, religious congregations, and university groups. Some have applauded, some remain indifferent, and some have been downright bored. But many others denounced me, even stormed out on me. On several occasions, entire congregations and audiences have exploded with rage because of my plea for justice and peace.

Once in 2001, I spoke to a packed Rhode Island Catholic church with Kathy Kelly, coordinator of Voices in the Wilderness, a nonprofit group that brought delegations to Iraq throughout the 1990s and early 2000s in a campaign to end the U.S. war on the Iraqi people. We spoke about the first Gulf war, the periodic

U.S. bombing raids, and the U.S. sanctions, which killed over half a million Iraqi children during the 1990s, according to the United Nations and UNICEF. I read from the Sermon on the Mount, then reflected on the Christian vocation to love our enemies, which I translated to include the people of Iraq. I told about my 1999 journey with Kathy and several Nobel Peace Prize winners to Baghdad and explained why those genocidal sanctions needed to be lifted, why the United States should cut all military aid to the Middle East, and why the United States should stop destroying Iraq and stealing its oil. Kathy spoke in greater detail, with more passion and eloquence, based on her many trips to Iraq over the years.

As soon as we finished, the congregation exploded. "How dare you criticize our government!" they yelled at us. "Who do you think you are? What gives you the right to criticize us or America? Why do you bring politics into our church? Our government's military actions have nothing to do with religion. You don't know anything about the cold, hard reality of war, tyranny, or terrorism. Keep telling us how much God loves us and mind your own business about our war." Some stood up and walked out in a huff.

Finally one gentleman demanded the microphone and explained that he had been the spokesman for the Pentagon during President Clinton's first term, that we were certainly well-meaning people, just terribly misguided, and that U.S. policy toward Iraq was not only necessary but justified. Everyone was greatly relieved, and the evening ended in disarray.

The church where we met that Saturday evening stood on a cliff overlooking the Atlantic Ocean, and for a moment I wondered how Jesus felt when they tried to throw him off the cliff. These devout, all-American Catholics were angry and insulted, just the kind of devout people Jesus faced in the Nazareth synagogue and throughout his life. His experience in Nazareth consoled me as I stood before that hostile Rhode Island congregation, and it continues to strengthen me every time people reject and denounce me for my stand for peace and justice.

According to the life of Jesus, this work of creating justice for the poor and reconciling peoples is the heart of the spiritual life. If we want to live an authentic, faith-filled life, we need to proclaim good news to the poor, liberty to prisoners, vision to the blind, liberation to the oppressed, the cancellation of the Third World debt, and the redistribution of the world's resources from the First World nations to the poorer nations, so that everyone on the planet will have food, shelter, health care, education, employment, and dignity. This is the work of Jesus. Because we are his followers, it is our work too. It will get us in trouble and lead us one day to the mountain of God in search of solitude, clarity, guidance, and peace.

To understand Jesus' message, we need to imagine what God's reign looks like, and what changes it requires. Because of his reading from Isaiah, we can conclude that, for Jesus, God's reign features justice for the poor, freedom for prisoners, vision for the blind, liberation for the oppressed, the cancellation of all debts to those held bound in poverty, and economic equality for all people everywhere. Luke writes throughout his Gospel that Jesus' vision of God's reign means the fullness of peace here and now for all humanity. Luke assumes that in God's reign everyone has everything they need, everyone lives life to the fullest, everyone loves everyone else, and everyone lives at peace with themselves, their neighbors, and God. Proclaiming

God's reign means healing people from disease, reconciling with enemies and adversaries, stopping all our wars, ending all injustices, refusing to cooperate with empires, and worshiping the God of peace. It means placing one's allegiance not with the state or its weapons or patriotic symbols but with the living God.

Jesus called his proclamation of God's reign "Good News," but I think we have lost the bold, political, even revolutionary overtones of this phrase. Whenever Caesar's troops conquered a new nation, Roman soldiers rode through the empire proclaiming "the good news of Caesar," "the Gospel of Caesar." This supposed "good news" could be summed up as follows: "We Romans have just killed hundreds of men, raped the women, stolen their goods, pillaged their land, burned their homes, crushed the opposition, destroyed their religious customs, and conquered the land. We have killed and wiped out a whole new region for Caesar, who is once again victorious. Hail Caesar! All praise to Caesar!" People were expected to celebrate Rome's brutal destruction. Caesar had declared himself to be a god, and they were forced to cheer his military victory or face similar destruction. Anyone who opposed Rome faced arrest, imprisonment, torture, and public execution. People were crucified regularly for resisting the empire. Because people lived in fear of being killed, everyone acceded to the empire's order. They did not know any alternative—nor could they imagine one. They were trapped under the vicious empire with no way out.

Coming into this political climate, Jesus' proclamation of "the good news of God's reign" is stunning in its daring challenge to Caesar, its bold vision of another way of life, and its radical hope in a loving, nonviolent God. It was nothing less than a declaration of independence from Roman rule. From now on, he announced, we are citizens of God's reign, and the good news is that God's reign is spreading, not by murder and war but by love and compassion, bringing justice to the poor and liberation for the oppressed through peaceful, creative non-violence.

No wonder Jesus was in such popular demand in this imperial outback! Few dared say such things in public. Few advocated revolution, much less nonviolent revolution in the name of a loving, living God. Jesus spoke with authority, his miraculous touch cured everyone, and his teaching showed a way to break free from the shackles of empire, fear, even death itself. Because Jesus' message was electrifying, the crowds wanted him to stay with them. Eventually they wanted to make him king, to bring about this revolutionary change right before their eyes.

But Jesus was a moving target. He was not under anyone's control. He was free. He lived on the road permanently, a pilgrim of peace walking through the world of war, announcing the good news of God's reign, denouncing the empire's injustice. Jesus wanted people to hear about God's reign and to welcome it into their hearts and lives. He was trying to build a nonviolent movement that would transform our hearts and lives, and in the process bring down the empire and welcome a new realm of love. He sought to liberate us from fear, violence, and death, so that we would live as God's beloved sons and daughters. His invitation into God's reign was widely rejected by the religious officials, and Jesus' life was in grave danger. As we too announce God's reign of peace and justice, and make clear the political consequences of this spiritual revolution—that the war on Iraq must end, that we can no longer fund the Israeli occupation of Palestine, that we have to feed all starving people from Darfur to Delhi, and that we have to dismantle our nuclear arsenal from Los Alamos to Livermore Labs–we too will face rejection, harassment, and persecution. Though our lives may be disrupted, our story will certainly resemble his story.

Teaching the Wisdom of Creative Nonviolence

Besides announcing God's reign, Jesus taught a new way of life in the world, the way of creative nonviolence. Matthew sets the context for this central teaching on a mountaintop, and we call it the Sermon on the Mount. Luke adds that, before he named twelve disciples as "apostles" and offered this great sermon, Jesus spent a night alone in prayer on a mountain. Both Evangelists sum up Jesus' teachings with the Beatitudes and the commandments of nonviolence: "Blessed are you poor. Blessed are you hungry. Blessed are you who weep. Blessed are you who are persecuted. Woe to you rich. Woe to you who are full. Woe to you who laugh. Woe to you when all speak well of you. But to you, I say, love your enemies, do good to those who hate you, pray for those who persecute you. Love your enemies and do good to them, and lend, expecting nothing back. Then your reward will be great and you will be children of the Most High, for God himself is kind to the ungrateful and the wicked. Be merciful. Be compassionate just as God is merciful and compassionate" (Luke 6:20–36).

Francis of Assisi once said that Jesus turned everything upside down. For Jesus, what we think is blessed is really cursed, and what we think is cursed is really blessed. The culture insists that riches, honor, food, and laughter are blessings, but in Jesus' eyes, they are curses. Jesus states unequivocally that the poor, hungry, mournful, and persecuted are those who are truly blessed by God. The culture curses those named in Matthew's Beatitudes–the poor, the mournful, the meek, those struggling for justice, the merciful, the pure in heart, the peacemakers, and those persecuted for their work for social justice. But Jesus announces that God blesses them. The broken, vulnerable, needy, and all those who work on their behalf for their justice, healing, and peace are blessed. The culture of war and weapons manufacturers curse those who make peace, but Jesus blesses the peacemakers and declares that they are actually God's sons and daughters. The culture of greed and domination curses the poor and the persecuted, but Jesus insists that God's reign belongs to them, not to the rich and powerful.

Although the Gospel invites us to stand with the blessed and become one of them, who among us wants to be poor, hungry, weeping, or persecuted? Who does not aspire to be rich, well-fed, laughing, and popular? Who dares love our enemies, bless those who persecute us, and do good to those who hurt us? This is the discipleship challenge of Jesus. Few practice this, much less teach Jesus' upside-down ethic. But his message cannot be denied, no matter how hard we try.

The Sermon on the Mount is the summit of his wisdom. No one in recorded history ever said these daring words: "Your country tells you to love your fellow countrymen and hate your enemies, but I say to you, Love your enemies. Don't kill them; don't nuke them; don't bomb them; don't sanction them; don't execute them; don't electrocute them; don't gas them; don't abort them; don't shoot them; don't torture them; don't oppress them; don't impoverish them; don't murder them; don't vaporize them; and don't assassinate them. Love them. Period." These are the boldest, most political words ever uttered.

To understand the story of the Transfiguration, we need to embrace Jesus' Beatitudes and his command to love our enemies. If we do not accept his sermon, adopt his wisdom of non-violence, and walk with him along the difficult road of universal love, we will never ascend the mountain of God with him in search of God's blessing. Because we are so steeped in the world's violence, it is hard to resist the patriotic lure of war and to accept such otherworldly values. But if we love Jesus and want to follow him, we have to accept his teachings, even if no one else in our families, communities, neighborhoods, or churches does. As his followers, we have to adhere to his strict path of active nonviolence, come what may. No matter how desperate the situation, how noble the cause, how loud the cry, how fervent the patriotism, or how terrible the threat, we will never hurt or kill another, and never again be silent in the face of injustice, poverty, nuclear weapons, or war. From now on, as disciples of the nonviolent Jesus, we are going to love our enemies—even if it kills us.

How do we love our enemies and practice Gospel nonviolence? We can love our enemies by reaching out to those condemned to suffer and die on our death rows and in soup kitchens, homeless shelters, AIDS hospices, and inner-city neighborhoods. We can love our enemies by publicly opposing our country's efforts to kill them. We can love our enemies by trying to stop U.S. weapons sales, military actions, bombing raids, and military spending. We can love our enemies by joining a peace vigil at a nearby nuclear weapons installation in a call for disarmament. We can love our enemies by siding with the children of Iraq, Palestine, and all those places targeted by U.S. bombs. We can love our enemies by "beating swords into plowshares" and "studying war no more." We may come under attack for this seemingly unpatriotic behavior, but we will find consolation knowing that we are doing what Jesus commanded and discover what it means to be blessed.

Jesus not only opposes violence, murder, war, and nuclear weapons, he not only refuses to justify war or bless war, he leads the way to a world without war by pushing us beyond national borders to this all-encompassing love for our enemies. Even more shocking, he commands this practice not just because it is the right thing to do, the moral thing to do, or even the most practical thing to do, but because this is what God does. We love our enemies because God loves God's enemies, and we are God's children, so we do whatever God does.

This great commandment is the only place in the Scriptures where Jesus fully describes the nature of God and how we can become more like God. God lets God's sun rise on the good and the bad, and God's rain fall on the just and the unjust, Jesus explains. If we want to be like God, if we want to please God, if we want to do God's will, if we want to serve God, if we want to participate in God's mission, if we want to share God's life, if we want to radiate God's spirit, if we want to be obedient to God like Jesus, if we want spiritual fulfillment in life, if we want to live our calling as the beloved sons and daughters of God, then we will love our enemies and show compassion to everyone just as God does. We will publicly love those whom our country condemns. We will risk persecution and rejection, but we will be blessed. Indeed, Matthew concludes, if we are denounced because of our adherence to Jesus' nonviolence, we should rejoice and be exceedingly glad, for now we stand with the prophets and the saints, and walk in the footsteps of Jesus himself.

"Jesus was the most active nonviolent resister known to history," Gandhi once said. "But the only people who do not know that Jesus is nonviolent," he pointed out, "are Christians." Gandhi read from the Sermon on the Mount every morning for decades. He knew it better than anyone. He saw it as the key not only to Christianity but to all social, economic, political, and spiritual change.

Likewise, Martin Luther King, Jr., said that the Sermon on the Mount is the key to understanding Jesus, the blueprint for all Christian living, and the best practical advice for ending racism, poverty, war, and nuclear weapons. The night before he was killed, Dr. King said that the biblical wisdom of nonviolence was the only hope for the world. "The choice before us is not violence or nonviolence. It's nonviolence or nonexistence!" Gospel nonviolence is no longer just an option, he taught. If we do not adopt nonviolence, we will destroy one another through global violence. All Christians therefore need to study and practice the wisdom of Gospel nonviolence. As we dismantle our weapons, feed the starving masses, and learn nonviolent ways to resolve international crises, we will finally obey Jesus' teachings and resemble the life of Jesus himself.

Serving the Poor, Turning Toward the Cross

After healing countless sick people, feeding thousands, even raising the dead, Jesus realized that his teachings on nonviolence and God's reign would be rejected and that, in the end, the empire would crush him. He turned to the disciples and asked, "Who do you say that I am?" "The Messiah," Peter answered. Jesus knew that they still did not understand his radical way of loving service and active nonviolence, so he told them not to tell anyone. He saw how they expected a strong, military leader who would overthrow the empire, create a new nation, crush all enemies, restore the house of Israel, and take over the world. But Jesus would do none of that. He would be a nonviolent messiah, the Suffering Servant foretold by Isaiah. He knew that nonviolent revolutionaries got crushed by Roman soldiers and their religious puppets. He could see the writing on the wall. "The Son of Humanity must suffer greatly and be rejected by the elders, the chief priests, and the scribes, and be killed and on the third day be raised," he announced solemnly to his disciples (Luke 9:22). They didn't understand a word of it.

For the first time in this astonishing story of healings, miracles, and parables, Jesus hits a somber note. He is not going to win the world over as they hope, at least not initially. He is not going to become a new emperor. He is not going to crush the pagans. Instead, he will be arrested, jailed, tortured, and executed as a criminal. Furthermore, he insists, if they want to follow him, they must risk the same failure and bloody outcome. "If anyone wishes to come after me, he must deny himself and take up his cross daily and follow me," Jesus declared. "For whoever wishes to save his life will lose it, but whoever loses her life for my sake will save it. What profit is there for one to gain the whole world yet lose their soul?" (Luke 9:23–25).

With this talk of arrest and crucifixion, the story takes a dramatic turn for the worse. Our hero is headed for a fall. Many walk away from him. It is precisely at this dramatic moment, as he explains how nonviolence requires a willingness to suffer and die in the struggle for justice without even the desire to re-taliate, that Jesus invites his friends to climb the mountain with him for a prayerful solitude.

Jesus knows his days are numbered. He sees the cross loom-ing in the distance. He realizes that his friends will run when his hour arrives. He understands that in a world of religious and imperial violence, his message of divine nonviolence will be re-jected, that he will have to face his final hour alone. So he turns again to his beloved God for strength to go forward in faith, hope, and love, that he might embody the divine wisdom of nonviolence.

As we begin again to grapple with the lessons and practice of nonviolence, the challenge of the cross, and the painful jour-ney ahead, Jesus invites us to walk him up the mountain of God.

QUESTIONS FOR REFLECTION

1. How do you imagine Jesus? What is he like? What episodes in his life touch you and move you?

2. How do you pray? Do you take quality quiet time every day to sit and be with Jesus? What would you have to change in your daily schedule to give priority to contemplative prayer? What does Jesus say to you in your prayer?

3. How can you begin to follow Jesus more and more in your life? How can you try to fit your life story more and more into his life story?

4. As you reflect back over your life, when was Jesus walking with you? What would it mean to start walking with him more and more now? What changes do you need to make

within yourself or in your life to walk more faithfully in the footsteps of Jesus?

5. How often do you read from the Gospels of Jesus? Can you put a copy of the New Testament near your bed, chair, or desk, and try to read a little of the Gospels every day?

6. How can you carry on Jesus' mission of announcing God's reign of justice and peace, denouncing injustice and war, teaching and practicing creative nonviolence, serving the poor, and taking up the cross?

Dear Jesus,

Please help me to walk in your footsteps, to accompany you on your journey of love and peace, and to notice how you walk with me through my life.

Help me always to be your friend, your servant, and your companion.

Give me the grace to become your disciple, that my life might reflect your life, that my story might be part of your story, that my journey might continue your journey.

Strengthen me to carry on your Gospel mission of announcing God's reign of justice and peace, denouncing injustice and war, teaching and practicing creative nonviolence, serving the poor, and taking up the cross. Amen.

PART TWO

UP THE MOUNTAIN
WITH JESUS

Steps Along the Transfiguration Journey

1. Take time out from your life journey to climb a holy mountain in a prayerful search for God.

2. Try to see the world, yourself, your family and friends, and the whole human race from God's perspective, through the eyes of unconditional love and infinite compassion.

3. Ponder your image of God. Try to imagine the peace, compassion, nonviolence, forgiveness, and unconditional love of God for you and every human being.

4. Make a list of the characteristics of a faithful disciple and companion of Jesus, and then try to embody those qualities. Envision your life as a faithful disciple on the road with Jesus.

5. Ponder how your life journey resembles Jesus'–from your birth and childhood, though baptism and repentance, to serving and healing others, teaching and praying.

6. Ask Jesus to accompany you through your life. Try to accompany him as he climbs the mountain of God to spend time in prayerful solitude and peaceful communion.

7. Try to follow Jesus by reaching out with unconditional love and infinite compassion toward everyone you meet and the whole human race.

8. Ask yourself, in every situation, "What would Jesus do?" and then do it.

4

Moses, Elijah, and the
Geography of God

In 1989, after working in a homeless shelter in Washington, D.C., for a year, I flew to Seattle to attend a peace conference before moving to the Jesuit School of Theology in Berkeley, California, to begin four years of graduate studies. At the end of the conference, some friends invited me to stay a few extra days to explore Mount Rainier National Park. I accepted their invitation, because I thought a few days of peace and quiet would do me good.

After a good night's sleep, they drove me to a park high up a nearby mountain, where they let me off along a path to spend the day hiking and meditating. Within minutes, I was alone in the silence of a mountain forest path. The contrast with inner-city D.C. was shocking. I walked for hours, thinking about my work among the homeless, my public stand for peace, and my upcoming move to California. I was leaving friends and family behind and heading into uncharted territory. I was on a new journey, but I suddenly realized that this journey was lifelong, a journey in the footsteps of Jesus into unknown territory until the end of my life.

I walked along the mountain path and mulled over my life. The beauty of the surrounding woods, the bright blue sky overhead, the colorful wildflowers, and the panoramic mountaintop view cast their spell upon me. Standing straight ahead of me, like a silent, benevolent giant, was the majestic, snowcapped Mount Rainier, reaching 14,408 feet high and covering almost one hundred square miles. The imposing snow-covered mountain filled me with awe and wonder.

After several hours of hiking, I reached a still, clear lake some 8,000 feet above sea level. Patches of untouched white snow lay about. The sunshine warmed me. I sat by the lake for several hours, looking at the mountain. But after a while, I realized that the mountain was looking at me! I became aware of my relationship with creation, and this led me to a deeper awareness of my relationship with the Creator. This Zen afternoon opened up a new space within me, where I could breathe deeply and feel at peace. Without my knowing it, the mountain was pointing me to the God who had created me and revealed that this Creator God was good.

From this mountaintop perspective, I realized that life itself and all of creation are good, and I felt the goodness within me as part of the goodness of God. Slowly the tensions and pains inside me began to settle down, like silt sinking slowly to the bottom of a lake, leaving clear blue water. There on that mountaintop, as a new peace floated up to the surface within me, I knew as never before the presence of peace, the peace of God, even the God of peace.

In comparison with the mountain, I felt as small as a grain of sand. I pondered the truth that no one could create such mammoth beauty and silent power. In front of Mount Rainier, I knew that God is kind and beautiful because only a good and gracious Creator could give us such breathtaking, magnificent sights. With every deep breath in that shallow mountain air, I was reenergized. I felt ready for the road ahead. Either the mountain or the God of the mountain was teaching me and pushing me forward on the mission of peace.

My friends picked me up later that afternoon, but it was only the next morning that I realized what had happened: I had been to the mountaintop. I had been granted a new perspective on life. I had received a taste of God's peace. This mountaintop experience gave me new strength to go forward to graduate studies in California, ordination as a Jesuit priest, and a public campaign for disarmament and justice. This mountaintop grace gave me the fortitude to respond three months later when six Salvadoran Jesuits whom I had known were assassinated in their home in San Salvador. I found new energy to organize dozens of vigils against U.S. military aid to El Salvador and, the following year, further protests against the First Gulf War. I could speak out against U.S. war-making because I had been to the mountaintop and beheld the vision of peace.

The mountain—and the God of the mountain—breathed new life into me. That experience gave me the power and energy to take new steps on the discipleship journey to justice and peace. From that point on, those steps became more peaceful and more focused. That mountaintop grace opened me to receive new energy to proclaim the Gospel in the most outlandish terms: that if we dare follow Jesus, we must abolish hunger, poverty, injustice, the death penalty, nuclear weapons, and war itself. With that mountaintop encounter, the God of peace pushed me beyond myself to announce the good news of peace in a culture of war. I was able to take up my mission, to be an apostle of nonviolence in a world of violence, a servant of the God of peace and justice.

Moses and the Mountaintop Mission

The mountaintop is the geography where God speaks to God's people and sends them forth on a mission to make peace and create justice. Perhaps the greatest story in the Hebrew Bible centers on the mountain of God. It begins when Moses notices smoke on Mount Sinai and decides to check it out. On the mountain, he prays and fasts for several days when he comes upon a bush that is burning but not consumed by fire. Suddenly he hears a voice say, "Take off your shoes, for you are standing on holy ground." As the story unfolds in the Book of Exodus, Moses becomes God's intimate friend. Eventually, God speaks to Moses, face-to-face.

From that first mountaintop encounter with God, Moses is given a mission. He is sent by God back down the mountain to confront Pharaoh and the empire and to liberate the oppressed Hebrew slaves. Moses is shocked by this request. He begs God to send someone else. Instead God promises to guide Moses along every step of the journey. Knowing that God will be at his side, Moses sets off to confront Pharaoh and demand that the slaves be let go.

After he leads the Hebrews to freedom, Moses climbs Mount Sinai again and once more converses with God. "If you hearken to my voice and keep my covenant," God tells Moses and the people, "you shall be my special possession, dearer to me than all other people, though all the earth is mine." Later, a cloud covers the mountain, and the terrified people see lightning, then hear thunder and a loud trumpet blast. Moses leads them to the foot of the mountain, when suddenly "the whole mountain trembles violently." Moses speaks to God, and God answers him, we are told, with thunder (Exodus 19:16–19).

On still another occasion, Moses climbs the mountain, just as a cloud appears and covers it. "The glory of the Lord settled upon Mount Sinai," we read. "The cloud covered it for six days, and on the seventh day God called to Moses from the midst of the cloud. To the Israelites the glory of the Lord was seen as a consuming fire on the mountaintop. But Moses passed into the midst of the cloud as he went up on the mountain; and there he stayed for forty days and forty nights" (Exodus 24:15–18).

According to these stories, the mountain is not only the source and base for political liberation but the geography of spiritual and communal transformation. After suffering through slavery and wandering in the desert, Moses and his people meet God personally on Mount Sinai. Apparently, we too need to seek the holy ground of God's mountain if we want to undertake the journey of social, political, and spiritual liberation.

Before they arrive in the promised land, God calls Moses to receive the Ten Commandments, which will serve as the basis for God's covenant with the Hebrew people. While Moses prays on the mountain, the people become restless, reject God, and create a golden calf. When Moses comes down the mountain and sees the idol, he throws down the tablets and calls for repentance. Later, when he climbs the mountain of God again, God passes by him, saying, "The Lord, a merciful and gracious God, slow to anger and rich in kindness and fidelity, continuing his kindness for a thousand generations, and forgiving wickedness and crime and sin . . . ! Here . . . is the covenant I will make.

Before the eyes of all your people I will work such marvels as have never been wrought in any nation anywhere on earth, so that this people among whom you live may see how awe-inspiring are the deeds which I, the Lord, will do at your side." When Moses comes back down the mountain, his face is radiant (Exodus 34:6–7, 10, 29).

According to Exodus, the mountain is the home of God, the holy ground where God speaks to God's people, sends them on a mission of justice and liberation, and teaches them how to live faithfully. The mountain is a metaphor for God and God's home. Today, the natural world, including the mountains, remains holy ground where we encounter God, receive our mission of justice and liberation, and learn how to live as God's faithful servants.

Elijah and the Mountaintop Encounter

Moses became the great lawgiver, who knew the God of the mountain and appeared to Jesus on Mount Tabor to encourage him to carry out his exodus. Likewise, Elijah was the greatest of the prophets, who also knew the God of the mountain. Throughout his life, he spoke out against the culture of war and the idols of death. In the midst of his campaign for faith and justice, he was led up Mount Horeb, where he met God, according to the first Book of Kings:

> Elijah walked forty days and forty nights to the
> mountain of God, Horeb. There he came to a cave,
> where he took shelter. But the word of the Lord came
> to him, "Why are you here, Elijah?" He answered: "I
> have been most zealous for the Lord, the God of hosts,

but the Israelites have forsaken your covenant, torn down your altars, and put your prophets to the sword. I alone am left, and they seek to take my life." Then the Lord said, "Go outside and stand on the mountain before the Lord; the Lord will be passing by." A strong and heavy wind was rending the mountains and crushing rocks before the Lord–but the Lord was not in the wind. After the wind there was an earthquake–but the Lord was not in the earthquake. After the earthquake there was fire–but the Lord was not in the fire. After the fire there was a tiny whispering sound. When he heard this, Elijah hid his face in his cloak and went and stood at the entrance of the cave. A voice said to him, "Elijah, why are you here?" He replied, "I have been most zealous for the Lord, the God of hosts. But the Israelites have forsaken your covenant, torn down your altars, and put your prophets to the sword. I alone am left, and they seek to take my life." "Go, take the road back to the desert near Damascus," the Lord said to him. "When you arrive, you shall anoint Hazael as king of Aram. Then you shall anoint Jehu . . . as king of Israel, and Elisha . . . as prophet to succeed you." (19:8–16)

On the mountain of God, the great prophet Elijah found God not in fire, power, or destruction but in the peace and quiet of a gentle breeze. Like Moses, he was sent on a new mission, back into the world to anoint kings and appoint prophets. He had been discouraged, but now he was reenergized. We can seek God on a holy mountaintop and discover God's mission for us. The challenge is to climb the mountain of God, like

Moses and Elijah, in search of God and our mission. If we dare, we too may come upon a burning bush or hear a still small voice, but according to the Scriptures, we will know that we stand on holy ground.

Everyone Needs a Mountain

Every one of us needs a mountain where we can climb above the struggles of the world to gain new perspective on life. From our mountaintop, we recognize our fragility and vulnerability and see the world a bit more as God sees it. We discover a new sense of compassion for ourselves, humanity, and creation itself. There on the mountain, we receive new strength and new clarity to go forward into the world on a mission of peace and justice. We too will receive the guidelines and teachings of God so that we can help others to reject idolatry and become God's faithful people.

Most of the saints and sages of history at one time or another retreated to a mountaintop to gain new perspective on life and encounter God. Gandhi journeyed to the Himalayas, where thousands of holy men and women continue to seek God today. After twenty-seven years in a Trappist monastery, Thomas Merton made a pilgrimage to the Himalayas to meet the Dalai Lama and other Buddhist monks and hear the voice of God in the still, small voice of Buddhism. Merton's official biographer even describes his life as a journey from mountain to mountain, culminating in the hill near the monastery where he built a hermitage and the journey to Asia and an untimely death. Like Elijah, Merton heard God's voice in the silence and became a prophet of peace to a nation of war.

On the night before he was killed, Martin Luther King, Jr.,

spoke metaphorically about his life journey as an ascent to the mountaintop where he looked over and saw the promised land of peace, racial equality, and justice. On April 3, 1968, he delivered an exhilarating and spontaneous speech that culminated in an audacious promise: "We've got some difficult days ahead, but it doesn't matter with me now because I've been to the mountaintop. I just want to do God's will, and He's allowed me to go up the mountain, and I've looked over, and I've seen the promised land. I may not get there with you, but I want you to know tonight, that we as a people will get to the promised land."

The theologian and civil rights leader Howard Thurman wrote in his autobiography that one of the high points of his life was a mountaintop expedition on which he unexpectedly and suddenly felt the presence of God as never before in the splendor around him. After that encounter, he carried on his work with an even greater vigor, passion, and clarity.

In 1943 the great Chilean poet Pablo Neruda climbed to Peru's lost city of Machu Picchu. As he wrote in his 1945 poem "The Heights of Machu Picchu," there he discovered "the old and unremembered human heart." All at once he felt compassion for the human race and dedicated the rest of his life to the poor and oppressed. On the mountain he had a spiritual experience and received a mission that he spent the rest of his life trying to fulfill.

At some point, we too need to climb a mountain, rise above our violence, see the world from the peace of a mountaintop view, and listen for the still, quiet voice of God. We too need to hear God speak and send us on our mission back into the world. If we want to engage in the nonviolent struggle for liberation as Moses did, or speak prophetically to the war-making world as Elijah did, we too need to climb the mountain of God. If we want to receive God's commandments of peace and non-violence, we too need to pray and fast on the mountain of God. We may not need to undertake a physical mountain-climbing expedition, but we certainly need to undertake a vigorous search for God, a spiritual pilgrimage to the holy ground where God will speak to us, instruct us, and send us forth. If we seek such holy ground, not only will we be sent on a mission but, like Moses, Elijah, and Jesus, we will be transformed and trans-figured to radiate God's light to a world of darkness.

5.

The God of the Mountain,
the God of Peace

When the peace activist Philip Berrigan and I were preparing with friends to walk onto the Seymour Johnson Air Force Base in Goldsboro, North Carolina, in December 1993, to hammer on an F-15 nuclear fighter bomber in a Plowshares disarmament action, Philip said to me that we do not need courage to undertake acts of nonviolent civil disobedience and risk years of imprisonment. We need something much deeper, much more difficult, much more powerful. We need faith in the living God.

I remember my initial shock at his insight. Later, when we walked beyond the No Trespassing sign, passed thousands of soldiers in the middle of national war games, and were arrested, tried, and imprisoned for long months in a tiny jail cell, I began to understand. I needed to believe in the living God, trust in the God who called me to make peace and end war, and place my hope in my abiding God to see me through my trials and imprisonment. Phil Berrigan helped me understand that faith is the key ingredient in our public work for peace and justice, in following Jesus on the path of global transformation.

Over the years, I have returned to his insight and tried to believe more in God, even though there might be little evidence of God's existence. I am constantly learning that the discipleship journey is a journey of faith. It requires walking in the dark, following the summons, going forward even though there is no concrete evidence of a holy destination. Walking in faith means acting as if one has faith. It requires taking bold risks for justice and peace on behalf of suffering humanity and the God of justice and peace, and, later, discovering the presence of the God of justice and peace and receiving the blessings for such obedience and fidelity. To be a person of faith in these times, therefore, is to be a person who actively resists every form of faithlessness, beginning with the idolatry of nuclear weapons and the mortal sin of war.

Faith, Not Faithlessness

One way to understand our global crisis of war, nuclear weapons, terrorism, corporate greed, rampant poverty, executions, and environmental destruction is to see it as a lack of faith. We do not believe in God. We do not believe that God is among us. We do not believe that God cares for us. We do not believe that God is a God of peace and justice. We do not believe that God can protect us from terrorism, war, poverty, anthrax, hurricanes, or nuclear weapons. We certainly do not believe that God is gentle, loving, and nonviolent.

If we did believe in the God of peace and nonviolence, we would not allow these atrocities to continue in our names or in

God's name. Instead, like Jesus, we would cross the line and announce the commandment of the God of peace: "Stop the killing. Stop the wars. Stop preparing for war. Stop maintaining weapons of mass destruction. Stop the poverty. Stop the corporate greed. Stop the executions. Stop the injustices. Stop the racism and sexism. Stop global warming. Stop the violence!" We would act as if the God of peace and love is in charge of the world, of our lives, even of our survival. We would do the things that God does, and trust the outcome to God's hands.

The classic image of humanity's encounter with God in the second chapter of the book of the prophet Isaiah teaches us not only how to get out of the madness of war–through our active disarmament–but how disarmament is the fruit of faith in the God of peace. In a few short verses, Isaiah sums up humanity's journey to peace as the journey up the mountain of God to the God of peace. If we journey up the holy mountain to God's house and meet God, we will be disarmed and journey back down the mountain to create a new culture of peace and justice. Our world will change because we have changed. We will have met the God of peace and discovered what it means to be human beings. From then on, we will live in faith and practice unconditional love, creative nonviolence, boundless compassion, and relentless reconciliation.

The prophet Isaiah wrote long ago that the nations of the world must climb the mountain of God. This is their vocation. There, on the mountaintop, God will instruct them in God's ways. They will learn what God wants them to do. Then, they will proceed back down the mountain, where they will immediately dismantle their weapons, share their resources with one another, and live in peace with one another and all creation. This text sums up the journey to peace:

In days to come, the mountain of God's house shall be established as the highest mountain and raised above the hills. All nations shall stream toward it; many peoples shall come and say: "Come, let us climb the mountain of God, to the house of God, that God may instruct us in God's ways, and we may walk in God's paths." For from Zion shall go forth instruction, and the word of God from Jerusalem. God shall judge between the nations, and impose terms on many peoples. They shall beat their swords into plowshares and their spears into pruning hooks. One nation shall not raise the sword against another, nor shall they train for war again. Come, let us walk in the light of the Lord!" (Isaiah 2:2–5)

Three Movements of the Spiritual Life

With this great text, Isaiah teaches the three basic movements of the spiritual life: climbing the mountain of God, encountering the God of the mountain, and journeying back down the mountain on God's mission of disarmament and peace. In the first movement, the nations of the world climb the mountain of God. This pilgrimage is the spiritual journey of humanity. All nations, cultures, races, and religions are called to search diligently for God. That search is like an arduous mountain climb. It takes preparation, discipline, effort, and determination. It is painful and requires faith and hope. We have not come close to realizing, much less beginning, this conscious global search. Yet as Isaiah foretells, one day the nations of the world, including the people of the United States, will realize that there is no meaning or happiness in money, power, consumerism, fame, revenge, presidents, the Pentagon, Wall Street,

Hollywood, or war. All nations will undertake the spiritual journey toward a Higher Power.

The second movement of the spiritual life is our encounter with the God of the mountain. According to Isaiah, when each one of us individually and the nations of the world collectively encounter God on the mountain, God will speak and we will listen.

Once we arrive on the mountaintop of God, our job is to listen attentively. This is the definition of prayer. Prayer is not so much talking at God, talking to God, complaining to God, yelling at God, or even praising God. Rather, prayer is a falling in silence at the feet of God and listening deliberately, consciously, attentively to God. It is not just letting God get a word in edgewise. It is allowing God to say whatever it is God wants to say to us. It is listening for God, taking God's word seriously, and deciding that, no matter what we may think, we are going to obey what God says.

According to Isaiah, as well as Jesus, the prophets, and the saints, God has a definite message for us. God wants to speak to us. God wants to tell humanity what God thinks. God wants us to disarm, practice nonviolence, and live in peace. Specifically, the text says that God will instruct the nations of the world in God's ways. The nations will learn on the mountaintop that God is a God of nonviolence, that God does not approve of killing, that God does not bless war, that God does not justify warfare, that God does not support retaliatory violence, that God considers our nuclear weapons as idolatry, that God condemns our nuclear arsenal, that God sees war as sinful, that God turns away from our violence, that God despises our imperial domination, that God wants universal peace, and that God desires all people everywhere to live according to the wisdom of nonviolence. Quite simply, when the nations of the world reach the mountain's summit, God will command them never to kill or wage war ever again. Instead the nations of the world will be told to live in peace with one another, with all peoples everywhere, and with the earth itself. This radical commandment will shock the nations because they define themselves by their power to massacre other people legally.

"From Zion shall go forth instruction, and the word of God from Jerusalem," we are told, "God shall judge between the nations, and impose terms on many peoples." God will instruct us, give us God's word, judge us, and impose terms on us. God will take action. God is in charge. God will be revealed as Teacher, Master, Ruler, Instructor, Commander, and Emperor. God will tell us what to do, and from now on, we will do it, individually, collectively, nationally, and internationally.

The third movement of the spiritual life is the journey down the mountain to dismantle our arsenals, create social justice, and promise never to hurt or kill one another or wage war ever again. After we climb the mountain of God and hear God's message of nonviolence, all nations will immediately undertake one specific political, social, and economic task: complete, universal disarmament. After meeting God, the nations of the world will pledge never to wage war again. They will beat their swords into plowshares, stop building weapons, and convert every existing weapon of death into an instrument of life. Spears used for killing people will be turned into pruning hooks that can be used to feed people. Instead of hurting and murdering others, these implements will help grow fruits and vegetables so that everyone everywhere will have enough to eat. Instead of raising the sword against another, threatening one another with war, bullets, chemical weapons, bombs, napalm, depleted uranium, or nuclear weapons, Isaiah says they will refuse to "train for war again." Once the nations of the world meet the God of the mountain, they will stop studying, funding, building, and preparing for warfare, and start acting like sons and daughters of God. They will know that God is a God of peace, and they will become people of peace.

Once we meet God and listen to what God has to say to us, our entire way of living, thinking, and being will change, not just individually but communally, nationally, and internationally. We will understand that we are all children of God, that every human being is equal, that no one is above another, that every nation is meant to serve every other nation, that the human race is called to reflect the love and peace of God. We will immediately set ourselves to the task of disarmament. According to Isaiah, all nations will commit themselves to nonviolence and agree to the terms of nonviolence outlined by God on the mountaintop. They will end every war, feed every starving child, and create nonviolent methods to resolve conflict. The root causes of war, including hunger, poverty, disease, homelessness, unemployment, illiteracy, and greed, will be eliminated. Everyone will be guaranteed sufficient food, housing, health care, education, employment, dignity, and fullness of life. All nations will embrace human diversity and variety with an all-inclusive love because, from now on, they will imitate the God they have met on the mountain.

Isaiah tells us that whenever we meet God, we are disarmed. If we encounter God, we will immediately stop our violence and start practicing nonviolence. If we listen to God, we will know that God loves peace and justice and we will work to create peace and justice everywhere. The atrocious lack of peace and justice in our world today, the widespread acceptance of war and injustice, the huge arsenals of weapons around the planet testify that we have not met God, that we have refused to listen to God, that we do not understand the nature of God, and that we disobey God's commandments.

The shocking revelation of Isaiah's testimony is that the God we expect to meet on the mountain—a God of violence, vengeance, and wrath—is not the living God we encounter on the mountain. To our surprise, we meet a God who is not like us at all. Atop the holy mountain, we come face-to-face with the God of peace, love, compassion, and nonviolence. We experience the goodness and loving-kindness of God, and worship the God of peace. Because we feel infinitely loved by this compassionate God, we eagerly listen to God's instructions on how to live in the world below. Once we experience the nonviolence of God, we realize that our primary task in life is to become people of nonviolence. Without wasting a second, we immediately embark on the mission God has given us, the social, political, economic, and spiritual transformation of the world into a new realm of perfect peace and unconditional love.

When the nations of the world meet the living God and realize that nonviolence is God's way, they will agree to be nonviolent with one another. It is this radical spiritual encounter with a God we do not recognize that leads us to dismantle our weapons, make justice for the poor, reconcile with enemies, and never wage war again.

If the so-called people of faith in the United States worshiped the God of Isaiah, the God of the mountain, the God of peace, we would not support war or allow war to be waged in our names, no matter how noble or compelling the cause. We would not pay taxes to support an immoral military budget. We would not occupy and kill people, including children, in Iraq or

Afghanistan. We would not maintain thousands of nuclear weapons, militarize outer space, or destroy the environment. We would not allow anyone to starve or suffer. If we believed in the God of nonviolence, we would dismantle every nuclear weapon, make restitution to those who suffer in poverty, close down every U.S. military base and U.S. terrorist training school, abolish the death penalty, feed every starving child and refugee, clean up the earth, and create nonviolent international peacemaking teams to solve conflict.

Because we do not believe in the God of peace and nonviolence, because we do not climb the mountain of God, because we have not listened to God's instructions, we do not do the works of peace. We do not practice nonviolence because we do not believe in the God of nonviolence. We do not live in peace because we do not worship the God of peace. We think incorrectly that God supports violence, vengeance, retribution, and war, that God must be just like us, that God is mean and deadly. We think that because we are violent and warlike, God must be too. But we have never met the God of the mountain. Our faith, hope, and trust are placed not in the living God of peace but in the false gods of weapons, the idols of death that we have manufactured to kill our enemies and maintain our unjust global hegemony.

Disarming Our Hearts

Isaiah and Jesus teach us that God is not like us in our preference for violence. God is not violent or warlike. Instead God is peaceful, nonviolent, compassionate, gentle, and loving. If we truly believe this, if we want to be near God, if we want to listen to God, if we want to be like God, if we want to be in God's company, if we want to be at peace with God, if we want to be united with God, Isaiah declares, we must renounce war. For Isaiah, and later for Jesus, this renunciation of war is the key to the spiritual life and the solution to all the world's social, economic, political, and spiritual problems. Jesus goes beyond Isaiah by commanding us not only to beat our swords into plowshares but also to love our enemies. He commends active nonviolence not just because it is right and just but because God is nonviolent and practices active nonviolence.

When we reach the top of the mountain and meet God, God will disarm our hearts and order us to disarm our arsenals. God will not condemn us, but God will command us. We will be told loudly and clearly to reverse our direction, take apart our weapons, institutionalize nonviolent social justice, and create a new nonmilitary, nonviolent, peaceful world.

Although we can easily dismiss this text as pious poetry, naïve idealism, or impractical dreaming, it stands as the apex of spirituality, religion, and the meaning of life itself. If we had the courage—the faith!—to take the text seriously, the world would be disarmed, transformed, and transfigured. So would each one of us.

Isaiah's image also explains the basic movements of prayer. Simply put, prayer is right relationship with God. Although God created us and loves us, we reject God, ignore God, resent God, fear God, pretend God doesn't exist, and hate God. But the spiritual life of daily meditation and fidelity leads us to friendship with God, even intimacy with God. Prayer is the attention to and ongoing development of our individual, communal, and global relationship with God. As we relate to God, we center our lives and the world in this loving relationship—and we find peace.

Isaiah's image of a disarmed world is possible only if the nations of the world live in right relationship with the God of peace. When the nations journey up and down the mountain of God, when they take seriously God's intention for humanity, when they live in loving relationship with God, they will act according to the ways of God. It is as simple as that.

These ancient words are not meant for ancient times or some other people. They are intended for us, here and now, beginning with those who read the words. In the end, the communities of faith around the world today, beginning with Christians, Jews, and Muslims, are most responsible for leading the nations of the world up the mountain of God to meet the God of peace and learn the wisdom of nonviolence. Government and military leaders will not lead this journey to peace. They will always maintain their dominating control, wage war, oppress the poor, and threaten the use of nuclear weapons. They will continue to worship the false gods of war and revenge, and lead us down the path of destruction.

Communities of faith and conscience, beginning with the Christian churches, can lead the way to making this text come true by refusing to cooperate with war and leading the peoples of the world up the mountain to the God of peace. If the churches are faithful to the God of peace, they must teach the nations not to wage war. They must not bless war, justify war, support war, pay for war, or engage in war. The vocation of all those who claim faith in God is to instruct the world in God's way of nonviolence and begin the process of nuclear disarmament.

The Witness of Ignatius and Francis

Two great saints who tried to fulfill the vision of Isaiah were Ignatius Loyola and Francis of Assisi. Both were pilgrims who sought solitude with God on lonely mountaintops and then spent their lives calling humanity to God's way of peace, justice, and love.

St. Ignatius referred to himself in his autobiography as the "Pilgrim." He had been an obedient soldier, a killing machine, and a wild womanizer until one day when he was struck by a cannonball and nearly lost his leg. While confined to bed for several months, he read the lives of the saints and decided to give his life to Jesus as they did. When he recovered in the 1520s, he gave away his possessions and walked across Spain to Montserrat, a high desert mountain some fifty miles from Barcelona, where hundreds of years before the Benedictines had established a monastery. After months of begging, walking, and sleeping under the stars, he reached the mountaintop, entered the church, and knelt down before the statue of Our Lady and her Child. There he remained in prayer through the night. Early the next morning, he took out his soldier's sword and placed it at the foot of the statue. He literally disarmed himself. Henceforth, he would be a pilgrim of peace. That mountaintop experience led him from violence to nonviolence and gave birth to the Society of Jesus.

After a Jesuit has been in the order for fifteen to twenty years, he is sent to a distant country for a sabbatical year of prayer and reflection. In the fall of 1997, I was sent to Belfast, Northern Ireland. Before reporting to the Jesuits in Belfast. I traveled through Europe for one month, visiting the holy places I had always wanted to see. I spent a day in the Carmelite chapel in Lisieux where St. Thérèse lived, worshiped, and is buried. I rode the train to Lourdes, where I led a Mass for peace, bathed in the cold spring water, and prayed for healing. Then I traveled to Montserrat to see for myself the statue where St. Ignatius laid down his sword and embarked on the journey of faith and nonviolence.

The monastery at the top of Montserrat still attracts pilgrims from around the world. A cable car takes you up over the desert above jagged, rocky cliffs to the monastery. After Mass in the crowded church, I joined the line of tourists and made my way to the small black stone statue of the Madonna and Child. I was moved to think of Ignatius praying alone before the simple statue. He literally enacted the vision of Isaiah. This leap of faith and personal disarmament bore tremendous fruit in the good works of the Society of Jesus.

From Barcelona, I took the slow train to Nice and Florence and on to Assisi. Afterward, I caught a bus to the foot of Mount La Verna in the Perugian fields. This mountain retreat was donated to Francis by a benefactor. Francis retired there to pray after his pilgrimage to make peace with a Muslim Sultan and after his community of friars minor began to reject his commitment to poverty and peacemaking. It was a long journey by foot from Assisi, but Francis liked the place's privacy and solitude. The last few years of his life were spent alone there. One day, while praying in a cave on the mountaintop, he saw a seraph attached to a cross fly down from the sky. Rays of light streamed from the seraph's wounds, and Francis found himself bleeding from stigmata. He died not long afterward.

Francis had retreated to the mountain of God to listen and pray. He felt that his life had been a failure, and his only comfort was the cross of Jesus, the symbol of perfect disarmament and nonviolence. His only friend on the mountain was Brother Leo. Francis read the Gospels, prayed ceaselessly, fasted in penance, and cultivated a spirit of peace. He wanted to be poor like Christ, to be peaceable like Christ, and actually to feel the love and pain that Christ felt in his body. On Mount La Verna, Francis's prayer was answered. Not only did he experience the pain of the cross through the stigmata wounds but he felt his heart widen with love toward everyone and all creation. Till his dying breath, he felt an all-encompassing compassion, as did the compassionate Christ, toward all humanity.

Francis too had once been a soldier, but he gave up violence to follow Jesus on the path of nonviolence. On Mount La Verna, Francis's heart was completely disarmed. Throughout his life, he fulfilled Isaiah's vision. He climbed the mountain of God, listened to the voice of God, and then walked God's way of nonviolence, becoming an instrument of peace. As a former crusader who rejected war, Francis eventually embodied the nonviolent suffering love of Christ.

After the bus left me off at the foot of Mount La Verna, I walked up alone to the monastery that stands where Francis prayed in solitude. The cave where he received the stigmata is now a small chapel. There I sat in silence and prayed that my heart too would one day be disarmed, that, like Francis, I would become an instrument of Christ's peace.

I wandered up to the park at the top of the mountain, where boulders lay between huge trees overlooking the Italian countryside. For hours I sat on the rocky cliffs, drinking in the breathtaking view. Suddenly, a huge wind came roaring up the mountain and nearly knocked me off the cliff. For a split second, I was terrified, thinking I would die. No one else was around, and I thought that, if I fell, no one would know what had happened to me. But I quickly regained my footing and my composure, took a deep breath, and felt gratitude for the experience. It put me in touch with the natural reality of La Verna, the rough mountaintop solitude that Francis would have known.

I walked down the hill at peace, filled with the Spirit, ready to dive deeper into Gospel nonviolence.

Like Isaiah, Ignatius, and Francis, sooner or later all spiritual seekers will climb the mountain of God, hear God instruct us in God's ways, walk down the mountain, dismantle the weapons in our hearts and in our world, and teach God's way of nonviolence. Sooner or later, we too will meet the God of the mountain, who will command us not to study war anymore and instead to create a new, nonviolent world of peace. As we walk down the mountain of God into the world of war, as we deepen our faith in the God of peace and experience God's merciful nonviolence, as we help our local faith communities disarm and teach peace, we will participate in building a global movement for disarmament that will one day abolish war and nuclear weapons forever. On that day, everyone will walk in the light of God and live in a spirit of love and peace.

Indeed, as Isaiah goes on to say in chapter 25, in the end, we shall all live with God on God's holy mountain. "On this mountain, the Lord of hosts will provide for all peoples a feast of rich food and choice wines, juicy, rich food and pure, choice wines. On this mountain God will destroy the veil that veils all peoples, the web that is woven over all nations; God will destroy death forever. God will wipe away the tears from all faces. The reproach of his people God will remove from the whole earth;... for the hand of the Lord will rest on this mountain" (25:6–9).

_____

6

The Uphill Journey of Discipleship

L ife is a difficult journey on the road to peace, but the Gospels testify that Jesus came to share that journey with us and, more, to pave new ground and point the way forward into God's reign of nonviolent love. After walking through Galilee serving, healing, and helping the crowds, Jesus deliberately turned and set his sights on Jerusalem. As he journeyed toward Jerusalem, Matthew, Mark, and Luke record that one day, Jesus took Peter, James, and John "and led them up a high mountain apart by themselves" (Matthew 17:1; Mark 9:2). So much was happening that he needed to get away and rise above it all for solitude on the mountain of God. Luke specifically adds that he "went up the mountain to pray" (9:28).

Most of us admire Jesus, but none of us want to undergo what he suffered, to make that journey to Jerusalem and that last, uphill climb to Calvary. In this age of pop stars and movie celebrities, we are, at best, fans of Jesus, not followers. But discipleship means walking in his footsteps from Galilee to Tabor then to Jerusalem, where Jesus turns over the tables of imperial injustice and faces arrest and execution. We may go to church, we may read the Gospels, we may respect his teachings, but to follow Jesus faithfully means to turn toward our own modern-day Jerusalems, resisting systemic injustice, putting down our swords, forgiving those who hurt us, and taking up the cross of nonviolent, suffering love in the struggle for justice and peace.

Since Jesus defended the poor, confronted injustice, challenged the ruling authorities, and broke every unjust law, his journey could only lead to a showdown with the imperial powers. Because we are his followers, our Gospel journey to peace and justice will also get us in trouble. Our discipleship to Jesus will lead us to love our neighbors, love our enemies, defend the poor, denounce injustice, break unjust laws, oppose war, and confront institutionalized violence with active nonviolence. Discipleship will disrupt our lives and take us down a path not of comfort and consolation but of pain and sacrifice. At some point, we too will want to climb a mountain in search of prayerful solitude with our beloved God.

Dietrich Bonhoeffer wrote long ago that the problem with Christians today is that we do not want to pay the price for following Jesus. We want "cheap grace," not the costly grace of the Gospel. Because we want cheap grace, we end up with all the trappings of church, power, ritual, and religious legalism, everything but Jesus and a living discipleship to him here and now in our own lives. If we dare become Christian, as Bonhoeffer wrote not long before he was arrested, imprisoned, and hung by the Nazis, we too will have to pay a price. We will have to study his life and change our lives so that we do the things he did and pay the price he paid. Discipleship will cost us, perhaps even our very lives.

"When we are called to follow Christ," Bonhoeffer wrote in *The Cost of Discipleship*, "we are summoned to an exclusive attachment to his person. Discipleship means adherence to Christ, and because Christ is the object of that adherence, it must take the form of discipleship. Christianity without the living Christ is inevitably Christianity without discipleship, and Christianity without discipleship is always Christianity without Christ."

To ponder the transfiguration of Jesus and experience our own transfiguration with him, we too will have to follow him on the path of public confrontation with the war-making authorities before we climb the mountain of God for a respite of peace. As Bonhoeffer might have said, we should not delude ourselves with the cheap grace of a false transfiguration. As with everything in the Gospel, climbing the mountain with Jesus and witnessing his transfiguration will be costly. But for the Christian, the price is worth it simply to be in the company of Jesus.

Unfortunately, life is so hard for all of us, it seems impossible to be as daring and noble as Jesus was. We may desire to speak out on behalf of humanity as he did but instead find ourselves struggling with marriage, children, illness, work, the mortgage, and our busy day-to-day lives. We may feel too depressed, discouraged, or hopeless to try to change the world.

All the more reason to follow Jesus up a mountain in search of prayerful solitude! Like him, we need to seek out mountaintop solitude and peace. We need something more than our country or television or the world can offer. Like Jesus, we need God. We need to rise above it all and get a better perspective on the world and our lives so that we can spend the rest of our days doing what God wants–serving humanity, loving everyone, and contributing to world peace. God's encouraging presence in such prayerful solitude is a great help for the Gospel journey of creative nonviolence in a culture of rampant violence.

When Jesus climbs the mountain, he is not going on vacation. He is not just trying to get away from the crowds. He is not looking for a resort and a spa. He does not intend to retire from the struggle for justice and peace. He is seeking God! He is completely focused on God and the mission God has given him to save the human race.

Jesus does not run away from the struggle. Instead, he runs toward Someone, and to our amazement and good fortune, he takes us with him. As we follow in his footsteps and risk public harassment for the way of nonviolent love and peace, we discover that, like Jesus, we too want to be with God more than ever. Like Peter, James, and John, we find ourselves led to a quiet place of prayerful solitude where God can speak to us anew. We too will begin to pursue God with the single-minded devotion of Jesus.

If we dare speak out for justice and risk our lives for peace as Jesus did, if we seek God with the same single-minded determination Jesus showed, even in the midst of the discipleship journey, we too will begin to pray and learn the benefits of contemplative peace. If we enter the prayer of Jesus, as Peter, James, and John eventually did, we too may one day hear the voice of God and find ourselves in the light of the transfigured Christ. With that enlightenment, we will be able to face the dark days ahead with renewed strength, deep faith, determined hope, and steadfast nonviolence.

QUESTIONS FOR REFLECTION

1. What does God want you to do with the rest of your life? What changes do you need to make in your life so that you might more and more fulfill Jesus' teachings of love and compassion?

2. When you have climbed a holy mountain in search of God? How do you take time out from your life journey to withdraw in solitude and prayer alone with God on the mountaintop?

3. What is your image of God? Is your God violent or nonviolent; unjust or just; mean and vengeful or loving and compassionate; warlike or peaceful; death-dealing or life-giving?

4. How would a loving, compassionate, nonviolent, forgiving God look upon the whole world, the human race, and you?

How can you begin to see the world through the eyes of such a loving, compassionate, nonviolent, forgiving God?

5. What does the God of the mountain have to say to the nations of the world today? How would God instruct the nations?

6. How can you help humanity "beat swords into plowshares" and "study war no more"? What blocks you from being more loving and compassionate, from working for peace and justice?

7. How do you identify yourself? What gives you your identity? What would it mean for you to see yourself first and foremost in relationship with Jesus, as a disciple and companion of Jesus? Are you willing to practice the costly discipleship that Dietrich Bonhoeffer wrote about?

8. How is Jesus inviting you to climb the mountain of God?

———————

Dear Jesus,

Please help me to accompany you as you climb the mountain of God.

Help me to walk with you, to share my life with you, and to see myself as your companion.

Help me to take quality quiet time with you in intimate prayer every day from now on, that we might have a true relationship and friendship.

Help me to know God as you know God.

Give me the grace to experience the unconditional love and infinite compassion of God, that I may begin more and more to share that unconditional love and infinite compassion with others, that I might "beat swords into plowshares" and "study war no more." Amen.

PART THREE

MEETING THE TRANSFIGURED CHRIST

Steps Along the Transfiguration Journey

1. Ponder those moments and times when you have felt the presence of God in your life, moving in you, touching you, acting in your life and the world.

2. Reflect on those times in your life when you felt the presence of Christ, and his light shining around you.

3. Reflect on those times when you noticed the light and presence of Christ shining and acting in the world.

4. Try to offer light in a world of darkness, peace in a world of war, love in a world of fear, hatred, and indifference.

5. Notice what part of you sleeps through life and what

wakes you up to the reality of God's presence, the meaning of life, and the truth of love.

6. Take quality time every day to listen to Jesus. Allow him to speak to you. Attend to his words of love, compassion, forgiveness, nonviolence, and peace.

7. Understand Jesus as God's beloved Son and yourself as God's beloved son or daughter.

8. Name the saints, prophets, and holy ones in your life who encourage you to follow Jesus on the path of love, peace, and compassion.

9. Name your fears, and hear Jesus tell you not to be afraid.

10. Allow Jesus to touch you and command you to rise. Ponder how you have risen. Practice resurrection, and live as if you are headed toward resurrection.

7.

_____

Jesus at Prayer

Prayer is at once the easiest and the most difficult thing we can do. What could be easier than sitting alone with oneself and God in perfect peace and silence? Yet it is precisely this up-close encounter with ourselves and the Great Unknown that makes prayer so uncomfortable.

In prayer, we face ourselves as we are, in our poverty and brokenness, alone with our illusions and delusions, helpless before the universe and our inevitable deaths. From our need, we turn to God for help.

Real prayer is humiliating. It is like a child sitting in a puddle of mud, calling out for help. Prayer means coming before God as we really are—broken, helpless, powerless, sinful, vulnerable, fragile, and weak.

But if we dare remain in the truth of our humanity and beg the God of mercy to have mercy on us, inevitably, a new spirit of peace and mercy comes over us. As our spirits lift, we receive new strength and grace, which carries us forward into the world, reenergized, reborn, transfigured in love, sent to love and serve others. Because of the experience of meeting God in prayer, we can face any danger, confront any crisis, and meet any challenge. In prayer, we learn that nothing is impossible with God.

Prayer is the intentional turning toward our own inner mystery and the mystery of God. The focus is not so much on the method or experience of prayer but rather on God. In prayer, we fall in love with God and discover that, long ago, God first fell in love with us.

Prayer is our attentive encounter with God. Through quiet prayer, every one of us can turn to God, speak with God, and be with God. Prayer is the key ingredient not only in the spiritual life but in becoming more human, more loving, and more compassionate. Prayer is the fullness of life because, ultimately, prayer is communion with the God of life.

The Daily Prayer of Jesus

Jesus practiced a regular, daily prayer devotion. The Gospels frame every major event in his public life within the context of prayer. Luke, for example, begins the public journey of Jesus with the image of him sitting by the Jordan River after his baptism in silent prayer. In this contemplative moment, the heavens open, the spirit of God descends upon him, and the voice of God speaks. "You are my beloved son," God tells Jesus. "On you my favor rests" (Luke 3:22). Suddenly, Jesus knows his true identity, the mission before him, and how to live his life. He knows he is God's beloved. This prayer experience drives him into the desert, where he is tempted to doubt God's affirmation but remains faithful. Those forty days were first of all intense days of contemplative prayer.

Jesus frequently snuck away into the hills to pray and be alone with God. According to Luke, the disciples would go off in search for him, only to find him all alone, deep in prayer, hidden in some secluded spot. On one occasion, he left at daybreak to pray alone, and when he was found, he announced that, contrary to their plans, he would set off "to the other towns, for this is why I have come" (4:43).

"In those days he departed to the mountain to pray, and he spent the night in prayer to God," Luke tells us (6:12). Jesus' silent, all-night vigil offers a clue to how he remained faithful to God and the journey of creative nonviolence. After this dark night of prayer, he appointed his twelve apostles and taught the crowds the Beatitudes and the commandments of nonviolence.

When the disciples returned from their mission announcing God's reign and healing those in need, Jesus burst out with a prayer of gratitude. "I give you praise, Father, Lord of heaven and earth, for although you have hidden these things from the wise and the learned you have revealed them to the childlike. Yes, Father, such has been your gracious will" (Luke 10:21). Jesus was a person of nonviolent action, but that was because he was, even more, a person of contemplative prayer.

The Deep Communion of Prayer

"Only in silence and solitude, in the quiet of worship, the reverent peace of prayer, the adoration in which the entire ego-self silences and abases itself in the presence of the Invisible God to receive God's one Word of Love," Thomas Merton wrote, "only in these 'activities' which are 'non-actions' does the spirit truly awake."

Apparently, Jesus' prayer was contagious. The disciples must have been impressed by his prayer. I imagine that, as they journeyed through the Galilee countryside, he would step away from the campfire or wander off alone in the hills, and when they found him, he would be sitting calmly, peacefully, centered in deep communion with God. They knew that something was happening to him, that this experience was important to him, that he needed to pray alone. Because he would emerge with words of wisdom and a miraculous healing touch, they may have presumed that his meditations in solitude and intimate relationship with God were the key to his power. They were right. They respected his prayer and his union with God, and they wanted to share it.

"He was praying in a certain place," Luke notes, "and when he had finished, one of his disciples asked him to teach them how to pray" (11:1). This suggests that Jesus had some kind of formal ritual to his daily prayer that the disciples dared not interrupt. Rather, they waited until he had finished his routine. So impressed were the disciples with his practice of prayer that they asked him directly, "Teach us to pray." His response sums up the Christian life and discipleship journey in a nutshell.

In the Lord's Prayer, Jesus teaches us to call God our "Abba," Daddy; to declare that God's name is holy; and to beg for the coming of God's reign of peace and justice and the implementation of God's will on earth exactly as it is done in heaven. He teaches us to beg for our daily bread. He tells us to ask God to forgive us exactly to the extent that we forgive others who have hurt us and thus commands us to grant clemency and forgiveness to everyone at every opportunity for the rest of our lives. He places the attitude and heart of forgiveness as the prerequisite of contemplative prayer. Finally, he urges us to beg God not to lead us into temptation but instead to protect us from all evil. Jesus could teach such a sweeping, all-encompassing prayer only if he had first offered it and lived it himself. His life was rooted in a deep communion with Abba, a radical obedience to God's reign and God's will, a regular forgiveness toward everyone, and a complete dependence on God rather than the world.

Jesus' actions show how he lived out the prayer he taught. Before he raised Lazarus from the dead, he offered a prayer of gratitude to God. At the Last Supper, he offered a long prayer asking God to glorify him, protect his friends, and make his disciples one. In the Garden of Gethsemane, he fell on his knees and prayed that he might not have to suffer crucifixion, but more important, that he might do God's will no matter what the price. "If you are willing, take this cup away from me; still, not my will but yours be done." He prayed "so fervently" and with "such agony" that "his sweat became like drops of blood falling on the ground" (Luke 22:42–44). As he died on the cross, Jesus offered a heartbreaking prayer of loss and abandonment from Psalm 22: "My God, my God, why have you abandoned me?" His last words were a prayer of loving forgiveness and perfect surrender. "Father, forgive them, they know not what they do. . . . Father, into your hands I commend my spirit" (Luke 23:34, 46).

According to the synoptic Gospels, in the middle of his journey, Jesus climbs Mount Tabor specifically to commune in prayer with God. He knows that he must walk to Jerusalem, where he will confront the ruling authorities, who will undoubtedly respond by arresting, imprisoning, torturing, and executing him. He realizes that he needs to get away from the crowds and center himself in his beloved God and God's will if he is to be faithful through this horrific martyrdom. With Peter, James, and John, he sits alone on the mountaintop and prays. When the three disciples fall asleep, Jesus remains wide awake, on fire with passion for God and the coming of God's reign of nonviolence. There on the mountain, Jesus is fully enlightened, fully aware, fully human, and fully divine. He is filled with the grace, love, wisdom, and peace, of God.

I imagine Jesus was absorbed in prayer for hours. He meditated in a deep communion with God. He was completely focused on God, the difficult journey ahead, and its only possible outcome—confrontation, crucifixion, and resurrection. Those hours on Mount Tabor, he knew, would give him the grace to walk the extra mile into the Temple and beyond to Calvary.

Jesus the Contemplative

Jesus practiced single-minded devotion to God. His prayer was simple and human but focused and trusting, centered and fervent. The Gospels do not describe Jesus spending his life sitting under a tree in search of enlightenment. Rather, he is constantly walking, talking, healing, admonishing, rebuking, calling, and teaching. He is surrounded by large crowds, attracting every type of person, from the poorest of the poor and the most abhorred outcast to the religious elite, the military, the wealthy, and the political leaders.

Jesus was a teacher, healer, peacemaker, prophet, and activist. But the Gospels suggest that his public action sprang from his secret, contemplative prayer, the profound spiritual relationship he experienced every day with his Abba. Like the disciples, we only catch a glimpse of Jesus' contemplative experience and find ourselves asking him how to pray. Jesus wants us to share that same deep communion with him, just as he shares a deep communion with Abba God. He wants us to root our active lives in a daily practice of contemplative prayer and meditation. The Gospels suggest that the only way to share his life and follow the discipleship journey is through this daily practice of contemplative prayer and communion with God.

As I ponder the private prayer of Jesus, I recall the legend of St. Francis of Assisi. According to the earliest biographies, Francis's first follower was his childhood friend Bernard. After the Crusades, his return to Assisi, and his illness, Francis renounced his father's wealth and moved into the ruins of an abandoned country church. One night, his friend came looking for him, and they talked long into the night about life, death, Jesus, and God. When they finally retired, Francis pretended to go to sleep. Bernard also pretended to sleep but secretly watched as Francis got down on his knees, stretched out his arms, and began whispering, "My God and my All!" Francis prayed like that until dawn. Bernard was so inspired by his friend's radical devotion that he quit his upwardly mobile lifestyle and joined Francis in a life of prayer, peace, poverty, and loving service. The prayer of Francis made all the difference.

Francis gives us a glimpse of the passionate, consuming, contagious prayer of Jesus. Francis was on fire with love for God. Jesus was perfect love for God. He maintained a steadfast inner peace and a burning heart of love for God, which led him into that mountaintop solitude of perfect communion and radiant transfiguration. There on the mountain, after years of deep communion with God, his body could no longer contain this perfect love. Jesus exploded with grace and light, and the disciples finally woke up.

8

The Light of Transfiguration

We are told simply that, while he is praying, the face of Jesus suddenly changes, and his clothes turn dazzling white, brighter than the sun. One minute he is standing there in ordinary, prayerful silence, the next he explodes with bright rays, like a supernova. He is no longer the person his disciples recognize. Now he is the glory of God shining in their midst.

Rarely do the Gospels feature such supernatural events. We read of dramatic miracles, awesome healings, spellbinding parables, even three spectacular resurrections. On one occasion, Jesus walks on water. On another, he calms a storm. But Jesus himself never changes–until now. More, his appearance by all accounts was not noteworthy. Jesus was in effect a homeless person "with nowhere to lay his head." When Judas led the soldiers to the Garden of Gethsemane for Jesus' arrest, he had to arrange a special sign—a kiss—to point Jesus out because he looked no different than the other poor, ordinary, ragtag Galileans.

But here, on the mountaintop, Jesus undergoes the ultimate mystical experience. His face turns into sunlight, and he is no longer recognizable. His clothes become dazzling white, a biblical description for martyrdom. For one brief, shining moment, Jesus becomes the Christ of God, as if the door of heaven opens and the divine light shines through him, dispelling the world's darkness. It is as if the spotlight of God were on him. All at once, Jesus is revealed as who he is: the God of light and peace. Luke adds simply that, when the disciples woke up, "they saw his glory" (9:32).

Jesus "was transfigured before them and his garments became glistening, intensely white, as no fuller on earth could bleach them," Mark writes (9:2–3). Luke records that "as he was praying, the appearance of his countenance was altered, and his raiment became dazzling white" (9:29). Matthew states that "he was transfigured before them, and his face shone like the sun, and his garments became white as light" (17:2). Both Mark and Matthew use the Greek word *metamorphothe*, meaning "to be changed." Jesus is somehow different. His appearance is awesome, amazing, overwhelming, terrifying, and exhilarating. He is the glory of God embodied in a poor, itinerant preacher.

By this point, the reader of the synoptic Gospels has begun to dread the outcome of the story. Jesus was clearly headed toward trouble. He had announced his impending martyrdom. The end could only be brutal and final. But here, we catch a glimpse of the epilogue. The story will not end as we expect. Indeed, it will never end. Jesus will live on. We can anticipate his resurrection because we now know that this itinerant preacher is not just a nonviolent revolutionary but the embodiment of the living God. Jesus is the glorious, beloved Son of God.

The Light of the World

We might wonder why Jesus turns into dazzling light. He could have turned into a ball of fire, a fountain of water, or a foggy vapor of mist. He might have become a huge dove or a gentle lamb. Perhaps he could have grown into a giant or turned into a large heart. I do not mean to be flippant. I wonder why the Gospels describe Jesus as the sun in a scene right out of *Star Trek* or *The Lord of the Rings*.

We find a clue in the Gospel description of Jesus as "the light of the world." "All things came to be through him and without him nothing came to be," the Gospel of John begins. "What came to be through him was life, and this life was the light of the human race; the light shines in the darkness, and the darkness has not overcome it" (1:3–5). Although John's Gospel does not include the transfiguration event, it describes Jesus more than the other Gospels in terms of light. When he came into the world, the evangelist says, it was as if God entered a dark house and turned on the lights. In his presence we could see one another and find our way in peace to God. John the Baptist's job was to "testify to the light. The true light, which enlightens everyone, was coming into the world" (1:8–9).

At the height of his confrontation with the Pharisees, Jesus announced, "I am the light of the world. Whoever follows me will not walk in darkness, but will have the light of life" (John 8:12). This is a fundamental description of Jesus as well as a short synopsis of the discipleship journey. We are in the dark, but if we stand with Jesus, he will be our light. If we dare follow Jesus, he will lead us to life by guiding us through the darkness of death. He will be our flashlight as we journey through the dark night of the world. With the light of Jesus, we are no longer in the dark. His light opens a way for us to live, no longer in fear, hate, or violence but in love and peace.

The transfiguration story portrays Jesus as being literally the Light of the world, enlightening everyone, giving life to everyone, guiding everyone through the darkness. "We have to do the works of the one who sent me while it is day," Jesus said before healing a man born blind. "Night is coming when no one can work. While I am in the world, I am the light of the world" (John 9:4–5). For followers of the Light of the world, the Gospels explain, the discipleship journey means continuing his work and becoming like him, the light of the world. In the Sermon on the Mount, Jesus states plainly: "You are the light of the world. A city set on a mountain cannot be hidden. Nor do they light a lamp and then put it under a bushel basket; it is set on a lampstand, where it gives light to all in the house. Just so, your light must shine before others, that they may see your good deeds and glorify your heavenly God" (Matthew 5:14–16). These verses take on new meaning in the dazzling light of the transfiguration story. As Jesus' disciples, we have to reconfigure our lives and undergo transfiguration as well so that we can light up the world around us. We are not to hide ourselves. In this world of darkness, the Gospel calls us to be the light of Christ. Like a bright city on a mountaintop, we are to light up the sky. From now on, we will live in the light, reflect the light, and radiate the light of Christ. We become instruments for his light to shine through us, so that others may find their way through the world's darkness.

The Light at the End of the Tunnel

While pondering this mysterious image of the transfigured Jesus, I recall the many stories of those who have gone through so-called near-death experiences. In many cases, they report how they encountered a Divine Being of Light, much like the transfigured Christ. Many books have appeared over the last few decades, written by Raymond Moody and other researchers, who have documented thousands of near-death experiences. Those people died physically and then came back to life a short while later. When their bodies technically died and the dying process began, many said they floated above their beds, then headed down a dark tunnel toward a Being of bright light who radiated total compassion and forgiving love. In the presence of this Person of light, they felt perfectly loved and at peace, something they described as otherworldly, literally not possible or achievable in our physical world. For Christians, this divine Being of light was Jesus.

I think these stories fit into the testimony of the Gospel. Jesus is called the Light of the world, and on Mount Tabor he turns into a light brighter than the sun. This is one of his many manifestations, and when we die, I believe we will enter the light of his presence, where we will feel his unconditional love, infinite compassion, and deep peace. In many of these recorded "near-death experiences," people felt completely forgiven. Their lives appeared before them. They were told that, if they wanted to enter the heavenly land of perfect love and peace, they had to ask for forgiveness from everyone they ever hurt, and had to forgive everyone who ever hurt them. For those who had fought in war, this meant suddenly meeting the people they'd killed and asking forgiveness. Because the peace, love, and joy were so overwhelming, everyone readily forgave one another in the hope of entering that heavenly place. Nearly all these dramatic, mystical stories revolve around the Light. Those who survived these near-death experiences were utterly transformed. Most strive now to live in perfect love and peace with everyone in order to prepare for their return to the Light.

"The light was pure and white, and yet it didn't blind me," Lois Erdman of Bismarck, North Dakota, said about her experience dying in a hospital bed (as told to Phillip Berman in *The Journey Home* [New York: Pocket Books, 1996]). "It was not like trying to look at the sun on a beautiful hot day. It was comforting, fine and beautiful. I knew that the closer I came to the light, that at some point the light would envelop me and I would be on the other side. But just as I was about to be enveloped, I was sent back."

"The light radiated a sense of peace and joy to me," George Rodonaia, wrote about his near-death experience, which led him afterward to become a Methodist minister (see Berman, *The Journey Home*). "It was very positive. I was so happy to be in the light. And I understood what the light meant. I learned that all the physical rules for human life were nothing when compared to this unitive reality. So I felt a wholeness with the light, a sense that all is right with me and the universe."

The most compelling of these near-death experiences is told by Dannion Brinkley in the best-selling book *Saved by the Light*. Brinkley was struck by lightning and died on September 17, 1975. He was revived twenty-eight minutes later. During that time, he encountered a "Being of Light" who reviewed his life with him and sent him on a mission of love and healing.

I looked straight ahead at the Being of Light, who stood before me. I felt comfortable in his presence, a familiarity that made me believe he had felt every feeling I had ever had, from the time I took my first breath to the instant I was sizzled by lightning. Looking at this Being I had the feeling that no one could love me better, no one could have more empathy, sympathy, encouragement, and nonjudgmental compassion for me than this Being. . . . As I gazed at the Being of Light I felt as though he was touching me. From that contact I felt a love and joy that could only be compared to the nonjudgmental compassion that a grandfather has for a grandchild. . . . I could hear the Being's message in my head: "Humans are powerful spiritual beings meant to create good on the earth. This good isn't usually accomplished in bold actions, but in singular acts of kindness between people. It's the little things that count, because they are more spontaneous and show who you truly are" (Brinkley, *Saved by the Light* [New York: Harper Paperbacks, 1994])

In these mysterious stories, we recognize the Being of Light as the transfigured Christ. Each testimony urges us to seek his divine light and come out of the world's darkness. The challenge focuses not so much on our deaths as on the potential for the fullness of life here and now. We are summoned to live every day as if we stand in the light of the transfigured Christ. We are to dwell in his compassion, forgiveness, love, and peace. In the process of living in the light, we begin to radiate his light and become like Jesus, the Light of the world. We dispel the darkness around us and act as mirrors for his divine light so that we reflect his light and shed light on the world's darkness. As servants of this Being of Light, the transfigured Christ, we share his unconditional love, infinite compassion, healing forgiveness, and deep peace with every person we meet from now on. When people enter our presence, they step out of the darkness and into the light. This is the lifework of every disciple of the transfigured Christ.

The Transfigured Christ in Our Midst

The transfiguration of Jesus remains a mystery. If we are honest, we must admit that we do not understand it and we cannot fully comprehend it. For a moment, we are told, he revealed the transcendent glory of God here on earth. All we can do is ponder it, meditate over it, contemplate it, and bow before the Mystery. But the story does tell us more about Jesus and who he wants us to become.

For Jesus, this transfiguring moment is the confirmation of all he believes and does. He had heard God call him "my beloved Son" (Luke 3:22) when he was baptized. Now he experiences that mystical truth in his own body as his face and clothes change into dazzling bright light. Jesus feels his vocation in his own person and knows he is the glorious Light of God. He must be greatly consoled. At a time when the rulers were plotting his assassination, when his disciples could not comprehend his mission, and when the darkness seemed to overcome his light, this mystical consolation fortifies him for the journey ahead. Now he knows that God is with him, that he is the Light of God, that God affirms his journey to Jerusalem, that the darkness cannot overcome him, and that he will live on in the light and life of resurrection.

Though we cannot fully understand the story, the Gospel invites us to believe that Jesus is the Light of the world, the embodiment of God, and the presence of peace. He is the dazzling glory of God standing before us. As his servants and disciples, we follow the light, lead others to the light, and dwell in the light of the transfigured Christ.

For the disciples, the sudden, miraculous transfiguration of Jesus was a shock and a surprise. Likewise, the Transfiguration challenges us today. We too need to ask ourselves: When have we suddenly realized that we were in the presence of Christ? Where do we see Jesus around us? Where does the glory of God and the light of the transfigured Christ shine in our midst?

St. Ignatius encouraged the early Jesuits to look for Christ in their ordinary daily lives. He told them to take time every day for spiritual conversation with one another, to discuss the presence of God in their daily lives. He wanted us to look deeply at our daily lives from a contemplative perspective and discover Christ in our midst. If we are attentive, he taught, we will see God in the creation around us—in the animals, ocean, sky, mountains, plants, stars, but most of all, in other human beings. Likewise, the Gospel teaches that Christ is especially present in the poor and in our enemies. Matthew's Gospel records Jesus' solemn assertion that he is physically present in the homeless, hungry, naked, stranger, sick, and imprisoned. What we do to them, he said, we do to him. God is present in the suffering, the ostracized, the marginalized, and the oppressed. In a world of widespread poverty, Jesus is everywhere. Jesus does not spend the rest of his life as a radiant, transfigured, enlightened Being of Light. Instead he becomes the Suffering Servant of Isaiah, covered in blood, racked in pain, dying as a criminal, helpless on the cross. Instead of "dazzling white light," Jesus adopted what Mother Teresa called the "distressing disguise of the poor." Though we may not see transfigured beings of light around us, we surely see suffering, dying people everywhere, from the tortured prisoners of Iraq to the oppressed people of Palestine and the malnourished children of the Sudan.

The transfiguration story suggests that, like the disciples, we may one day suddenly realize we are in the presence of Christ. Whether we find Christ in the broken people around us, the beauty of creation, the struggle for justice and peace, the sufferings of the poor, the love of our enemies, or the breaking of the bread, we will recognize the light of Christ shining in our midst. In those moments, we are transformed by the Light falling on us. We will understand ourselves as children of the Light, servants of the Light, and instruments of the Light. We will feel the love, forgiveness, and compassion of the transfigured Christ enlightening us. We will reject the world's darkness, with all its violence, fear, hostility, and wars, and find new hope, purpose, and meaning in his light. Suddenly we will be disarmed and feel the peace of the transfigured, risen Christ. Without having to undergo a near-death experience, we too will want to spend the rest of our lives seeking his light, sharing his light, and living in his light. From now on, we will always want to dwell in the light of the transfigured Christ.

_____

9

Talking About the Cross

Matthew and Mark tell us that Moses and Elijah appear next to the transfigured Jesus. They represent the law, the prophets, the Hebrew Scriptures, and Judaism itself, and they are "talking" with Jesus as he stands in glory.

Then Luke adds a key phrase. They "appeared in glory and spoke of his departure, which he was to accomplish at Jerusalem" (9:31). Other translations state that they "spoke of his exodus that he was going to accomplish in Jerusalem."

In other words, they are talking about the cross. They have not come as tourists to look at the view from atop the mountain. They have not come to impart their wisdom to the disciples. They do not draw attention to themselves. They have come for one specific purpose: to encourage Jesus as he embarks on his journey to Jerusalem, where he will confront systemic injustice; undergo arrest, imprisonment, torture, and brutal execution on a cross; and in doing so, save humanity through his nonviolent, suffering love.

Of all the people to appear to Jesus! King David does not come to Mount Tabor. Solomon does not show up. None of the brutal leaders of old come by to encourage Jesus. Instead, we find Moses, the great liberator of the Hebrew slaves, conversing with Jesus, along with the greatest of all the prophets, Elijah.

The Evangelists frame Jesus' political march of nonviolent resistance into Jerusalem within the context of the law and the prophets. Jesus fulfilled the law of Moses and the prophecies of Elijah and his successors, they explain. Moses and Elijah stand by him to underline the spiritual truth that nonviolent resistance, unearned suffering, and martyrdom are God's will. The way of the cross is the way to God. It is the new exodus, the ultimate liberation, and the greatest act in history. On the cross, Jesus will fulfill God's mission of transforming nonviolence and lead billions into God's reign of peace.

The most touching aspect of this dramatic scene on Mount Tabor lies in the heart of Jesus himself. Surely each one of us needs convincing that the cross of nonviolence is God's way, but according to the synoptic Gospels, Jesus too needed such encouragement. Moses and Elijah console Jesus with their presence. They encourage him and urge him on. Their solidarity confirms his destiny, the upcoming political confrontation and his subsequent execution. Their presence affirms the redemptive, salvific, and eternal consequences of his martyrdom. He will be the ransom that releases humanity from the power of death. His perfect nonviolence will free humanity from its slavery to violence.

Later, after his resurrection, Jesus will tell his stunned disciples on the road to Emmaus that his martyrdom was the fulfillment of the law and the prophets. But here on the mountaintop, he hears this message for himself from Moses and Elijah. Their lives point to his mission and salvific work, including his seemingly disastrous end at the hands of the imperial military. The reader of the Gospels now knows that Jesus is not acting on a whim. Rather, his journey is the fulfillment of the Hebrew pilgrimage, indeed the peak experience and climax of human history.

Jesus had spent the previous months practicing active nonviolence, teaching his disciples to love their enemies, and rebuking them when they wanted, instead, to call down hellfire on their opponents. He told them to be as compassionate as God, instructing them to forgive one another every day, every hour if necessary, in order to keep building community. Most of all, he insisted that God is a generous parent, wildly in love with every human being, dying to share with us the fullness of life and peace.

With the appearance of Moses and Elijah on Mount Tabor, Jesus becomes the fulfillment of God's peace and compassion. He is the law and the prophet of nonviolence. In a world of war, executions, greed, imperial power, military might, widespread oppression, and genocidal violence, the transfigured Jesus becomes the glorious God of nonviolence. Moses and Elijah affirm that his active nonviolence is the height of Godliness and the hope of the human race. As they converse with the glorified, transfigured Jesus, they know better than any of us that Jesus embodies not only the law and the prophets but the God of peace and nonviolence.

The Cross of Nonviolent Resistance

I think we all need to start talking about the cross as Moses, Elijah, and Jesus did on Mount Tabor. Church people today seem to talk about everything but the cross. If we were on Mount Tabor, the cross would probably be the last thing we would talk about. We would discuss the light and glory of Jesus, debate the finer points of the law with Moses, ponder the lessons of Elijah, comment on the beautiful view, or focus on our own personal problems. They, by contrast, get right to the heart of the matter. They address the upcoming passion and death of Jesus and what it means in the context of salvation history.

We too need to talk about the cross, even if that means letting our questions and doubts rise within us: How can the cross be God's way to disarm, transform, and redeem humanity? How can the brutal execution of a gentle itinerant rabbi save the world, much less overcome Roman militarism and all the empires that follow? How can the cross be the culmination of God's visit to the human race, the outcome of such a heroic, virtuous life? How can the cross be the way for Jesus—and for us—to fulfill the spiritual life?

As we ask these questions, we might wonder what alternative Jesus had. Should he have stayed in Galilee, taught the masses, enjoyed the accolades, and lived to a ripe old age, while the Roman Empire rolled over the world's poor with the help of religious leaders everywhere? No. As humanity's Good Shepherd, Jesus had no choice but to protect us from imperial foxes and military wolves. He could not sit back and enjoy life while so many suffered unjustly and died under the heels of the ruling authorities. How could humanity ever find hope in him, the God of peace, if he lived quietly and comfortably while God's people suffered under oppression, injustice, and war? Jesus' silence would have meant complicity with imperial violence. He had to take action and risk his life. He had to offer the greatest act of nonviolent love the world has ever seen.

Jesus had to act. He knew from firsthand experience that the slightest outburst, the simplest political critique in his war-torn homeland would result in immediate Roman retaliation, even arrest and crucifixion. No one stood a chance against the Roman military authorities and their religious sycophants. In such a world, the best he could do was choose not only how to live but how, where, and when to die. He would give his life in nonviolent resistance to this culture of war and death, and his death would be a gift and an inspiration to humanity. More, it would be the redemption of all. He called his followers to join him on this permanent campaign of revolutionary nonviolence.

The Jerusalem Temple was the symbol not only of God's presence but of Roman and religious oppression. In order to worship God, the devout had to make an annual pilgrimage at Passover time, exchange their money for Temple coins, pay the expensive Temple tax, and buy the sacrificial offering (such as a pigeon). According to religious authorities, this purchase was the only authentic worship available. Instead of welcoming the pilgrims into a holy sanctuary of contemplative prayer before the God of peace, the Temple institution robbed the faithful of their meager income in one of history's ultimate scams. By co-operating with the Roman Empire, the religious authorities profited from this injustice, all in God's name. If the faithful did not pay their dues in the Jerusalem Temple, they faced being ostracized, if not excommunicated.

For Jesus, the unjust Temple system was the ultimate heart-break. As God's representative, he had no choice but to confront the system head-on, in God's name, and say, "Enough!" He would walk to Jerusalem, enter the Temple, turn over the tables of the money changers, dismiss the cattle, prevent the businessmen from conducting their trade, and denounce this "den of robbers" as an affront to God. He would not hurt or kill anyone, but he would engage in provocative, peaceful, public nonviolent direct action. He would give his life for true worship of the God of life.

Jesus' illegal civil disobedience could have only one outcome: arrest and execution. Political revolutionaries in Jesus' day were crucified publicly to deter others from similar resistance. Nonviolent protesters under repressive regimes everywhere– in apartheid South Africa, British-run India, U.S.-bombed El Salvador–know that such action is nothing less than revolutionary and will not be tolerated. Rulers know better than any of us that, if ordinary people of faith and conscience start engaging in dramatic, public civil disobedience and nonviolent noncooperation with their oppressive policies, their ruling days are numbered. Sooner or later, the masses will lose their fear, be emboldened with faith, walk forward in hope, refuse to cooperate with military occupation and systemic injustice, and publicly demand a change. Yes, the authorities will respond, initially by dismissing such noncooperation, ultimately through massive repressive violence, but eventually, in the face of steadfast, active nonviolence, they will be converted and the structures of violence will be disarmed.

Jesus saw all this from his mountaintop perch. He read the signs of the times and could see the road ahead. He knew how brutal the ruling powers were and how costly his nonviolence would be. But he also knew that his dramatic action and public execution were the greatest gift he could offer the human race. From the cross, Jesus would declare, "The violence stops here in my body. All is forgiven. Stop the killing. Stop the injustice. Stop hurting one another. Repent of your violence. Welcome, the nonviolent reign of God." His death would be the most perfect act of nonviolence in human history, and it would touch every human being's heart for all time, even if we did not know it. He would epitomize the dynamic of nonviolence, the greatest example of ultimate love, laying down one's life selflessly for suffering humanity and, through this martyrdom, disarming countless human hearts and even the Roman Empire itself.

Nonviolence, the Only Way Forward

Moses and Elijah understand that God is a God of truth and suffering love, a God of compassion and nonviolence, a God of action who cannot sit by while people are oppressed in his name. When they appear to Jesus atop Mount Tabor, they confirm what Jesus sees: nonviolent resistance and crucifixion will be his ultimate exodus. He will achieve not merely the liberation of several million people from Egyptian slavery, an awesome accomplishment if ever there was one. Rather, he will accomplish the liberation of the entire human family from the slavery of violence, war, and death, and show us how to live and die by loving one another with perfect nonviolence and heartfelt compassion toward every other human being. Jesus' life and death will touch every human being who ever lived, all 110 billion people. Deep down, few human hearts can remain unmoved by his selfless love, daring nonviolence, complete forgiveness, and sacrificial death. At the hour of death, even the hardest hearts call out to him for mercy and help.

The cross then is the way forward for Jesus and for anyone who wishes to pursue his vision of love and peace. None of us can sit by idly while the world consumes itself with violence and war. Each one of us—if we want to pursue the morality and sanctity of Christ, if we want to plumb the depths of the spiritual life—must engage in some public nonviolent action for justice and disarmament. Sooner or later, we too will turn deliberately toward our own modern-day Jerusalems and confront the culture of war and injustice. We too will have to speak out against killings, executions, racism, poverty, war, nuclear weapons, corporate globalization, and environmental destruction through public, nonviolent action. We too will have to face our culture's preference for violence, and suffer the consequences for our noncooperation with systemic injustice.

Dr. King explained it best: "Unearned suffering is redemptive." In 1963, when he and thousands of others demonstrated in Birmingham, Alabama, for civil rights, marched through the city park in violation of a court injunction, and suffered under the fire hoses and German shepherds of Bull Connor and his (all-white) police force, the whole country was appalled yet inspired by unarmed, innocent citizens who, although attacked for their peaceful march and just cause, continued to walk with dignity, civility, and truth. Their acceptance of suffering, insistence on the truth of racial equality, and nonviolent demeanor opened the eyes of millions of white people to the rightness of racial equality, through shared humanity. Not only did the media, president, and Congress move forward on a civil rights bill but the firemen, ashamed of their brutal behavior, could no longer unleash their hoses when the people came back for more; the nonviolent marchers were allowed to pass right through their lines of defense. A similar scene occurred when unarmed nuns and students blocked the streets of Manila in *1986* to protest Ferdinand Marcos's dictatorship. The Filipino soldiers did not dare open fire on these unarmed people. Rather, one by one, the generals and soldiers joined the protesters until Marcos fled the country. Nonviolence, as such demonstrations teach, always works.

The willingness to suffer without striking back while continuing to insist on the truth of justice and peace is the essence of love and disarms the hearts of our opponents without their knowing it. Dr. King said we need to match the suffering inflicted on the poor and our nation's enemies with our own willingness to suffer in their defense, even to go to jail and die if necessary for the cause of justice and peace. If we suffer for a just cause but maintain our dignity and respect while insisting on the truth of our cause and the potential for our adversaries to be converted, we will wear them down with our love and eventually win over the world to our cause. In nonviolence, the victory of justice is assured. It is guaranteed. In the transfiguration of Jesus, we see the final outcome–the light and glory of resurrection.

The Logic of the Cross

Jesus' willingness to suffer and be killed for his prophetic call and nonviolent action for justice is the epitome of active, loving nonviolence. The cross of Christ was the perfect manifestation of love and truth pitted against imperialism, militarism, and religious corruption. As far as everyone was concerned, the initial, horrible outcome was a complete disaster. Jesus was crushed. His cause, his vision, his life was defeated.

But Jesus eventually won. Even if most human beings are repelled by organized religion, hypocritical church officials, and TV evangelists, everyone admires and likes the nonviolent Jesus. He was the gentlest, wisest person who ever lived. People instinctively know his gentleness, truth, and nonviolence first and foremost because of the purity and forgiving love of his martyrdom. The logic of the cross, as the theologian Jim Douglass explains, is that it breaks open our hearts, disarms us and our opponents, and slowly transforms the whole world into God's reign of peace, justice, and love. In the end, the nonviolent Jesus will win us all over, and as John's Gospel states, he will "draw all to himself."

"Nonviolence in its dynamic condition means conscious suffering," Gandhi once wrote. "It does not mean meek submission to the will of the evildoer, but it means the pitting of one's whole soul against the will of the tyrant. Working under this law of our being, it is possible for a single being to defy the whole might of an unjust empire to save his honor, his religion, his soul and lay the foundation for that empire's fall or regeneration."

When Moses and Elijah appear to Jesus and discuss his exodus, they confirm the logic of the cross and deny the logic of war, power, empire, oppression, and murder. Violence never improves anything. Rather, violence always leads to further violence. It makes everything worse. The cross of nonviolence, by contrast, breaks the cycle of violence through our insistence on the truth of justice and our refusal to strike back with further violence. Now, for the first time, people are freed from their slavery to the culture of violence and can reach out to one another with love and compassion. There is no reason to keep on fighting. Even when the oppressors try to murder everyone, one day they will see the pain they have caused and repent. No matter how noble the cause or the fervor of the culture's patriotism, people of nonviolence refuse to support war. They insist on loving every human being on the planet, even those labeled enemies, and so they will refuse to kill or support the killing of anyone. The way of the cross, the way of nonviolence, wears us all down, so that one day we will look into one another's eyes and recognize ourselves as sisters and brothers, as equal children of the God of peace.

Nonviolence is the way of God, and as a law of nature, it always works, even when it appears–temporarily–to fail. Sooner or later, in God's good time, nonviolence disarms, transforms, and brings forth the good fruit of peace and justice. It cannot do otherwise. With the God of nonviolence, all things are possible.

For Jesus, the path of nonviolence was already confirmed in the astonishing presence of the two greatest figures in his history, Moses and Elijah. With this encounter and spiritual conversation, Jesus felt new energy to go down the mountain and face the ruling authorities in the spirit of divine nonviolence. Just as he found consolation from Moses and Elijah, we can find strength from the great prophets of nonviolence in our own times, such as Martin Luther King, Jr., Mahatma Gandhi, Dorothy Day, Thomas Merton, Rosa Parks, and Daniel and Philip Berrigan. If we dare listen to them, study their message, and hear their advice, we, like Jesus, will find the strength to carry on the journey of nonviolence to our own modern-day Jerusalems.

Jesus is not alone as he faces the cross. Moses and Elijah stand by him with words of wisdom, affirmation, and encouragement. Jesus knows that God has not abandoned him. He can march on, come what may.

But what about the disciples? There they lie, in the midst of his glory, sound asleep. They missed the entire conversation among Jesus, Moses, and Elijah. They offer no support to Jesus as he faces his journey to the cross. Instead, they snore away, enjoying the comfort of their mountaintop retreat. They are in for a great awakening. So are we.

10.

_____

Sleeping Through the Transfiguration

The Gospel of Luke records that Peter, James, and John were "overcome with sleep" and slept through Jesus' transfiguration. Presumably, they were exhausted from the endless walking, the crowds, and the mountain climb. As soon as Jesus started to pray, they fell asleep. Later, the same three disciples will fall asleep repeatedly in the Garden of Gethsemane on the Mount of Olives, where Jesus agonizes over his impending arrest and execution on the cross.

The image is deliberate. Jesus has just announced that he is going to Jerusalem, where he will be killed for his nonviolent resistance, and instead, the disciples ask if they can call down hellfire on their enemies and then debate which among them is the greatest. If the story were not so tragic, the disciples would appear as dim-witted and hilarious as the Keystone Kops, the Three Stooges, and the Marx Brothers all rolled into one.

The image of the sleeping disciples is shocking, sad, and instructive. It is as if the Evangelists were saying, right from the beginning, that the early community could not grasp the urgent spiritual gift they were offered. Instead of staying awake with Jesus through the dark night of resistance, they turned away. Instead of witnessing his transfiguration, they fell sound asleep. Instead of supporting Moses and Elijah as they encouraged Jesus carry the cross, they snored soundly.

The image helps explain today's male-dominated, institutional Church. For two thousand years, churchmen have slept through an enormous array of astonishing transfigurations, those social movements for peace and justice that have shown the glory of God working in our tragic world, from St. Francis's movement of voluntary poverty and antifeudal, personal disarmament through Gandhi's movement for India's independence to Archbishop Tutu's South African campaign to abolish apartheid. By and large, the institutional Church has been oblivious to God's ongoing social transformation of humanity. In our silence and complicity, we have slept tight while God revealed the glory of Christ in the liberation of the poor and oppressed. To make matters worse, the Church has often criticized, hindered, and opposed nonviolent movements for social change.

When I reflect on history's great movements for peace and justice, I do not see male church leaders (especially Catholic leaders) at the forefront, whether in the abolitionist and suffragist movements or the labor and civil rights movements or the antiwar and environmental movements. For decades in the U.S. Catholic community, Dorothy Day was the lone voice for peace. She faced constant harassment and criticism from priests, bishops, and cardinals. Male churchmen denounced her and the Catholic Worker, as well as all the great prophets of the last century, from Franz Jägerstätter and Mahatma Gandhi, through

Martin Luther King, Jr., and Oscar Romero, to Fannie Lou Hamer and Ita Ford.

One could almost conclude that, since Constantine welcomed Christians into the empire and its wars, churchmen have rejected Jesus' nonviolent pursuit of justice and peace, the way of the cross, for the last seventeen hundred years. Rather, they were fascinated by imperial power, the just war theory, their growing bank accounts, their real estate, their lawyers, and their control over the Church. In other words, they continue to sleep through the presence and glory of God.

Perhaps the recent scandals of pedophile priests and hierarchical cover-ups best expose the somnolence of the institutional, male-dominated Catholic Church. The crimes and cover-ups have been appalling. That one child, much less hundreds or even thousands, was ever hurt is unconscionable. That children and young people were hurt by priests who were supposed to be serving them, and that the Church covered up these abuses for decades, constitutes a grave injustice. That the Church has yet to repent, open discussions within its wide community, and welcome women and the laity into positions of authority is mind-boggling and heartbreaking.

Like everyone, I was deeply saddened by the violence and pain committed by churchmen, and with everyone in the Church, I apologize to anyone who has been hurt. I hope that the Church wakes up and makes sure this violence never happens again, that our Church rejects its love of power, domination, secrecy, and sexism, and becomes the community of peace and nonviolence that Jesus intended.

If the Church is finally to become a community of peace and nonviolence, following in the footsteps of its nonviolent founder, then it must of course ordain women and married people, and include everyone in its embrace. It must always side with the poor and the oppressed in the struggle for justice. Otherwise, it will continue to oppose the mission of Jesus. The Church must always stand with the world's children, the first to suffer famine, oppression, and war.

The acid test of the Church's transformation, even transfiguration, will be its final rejection of the so-called just war theory, its active opposition to war and militarism, and its complete embrace of Gospel nonviolence. Until the Church repents of its Constantinian betrayal and absolutely rejects its support of war and nuclear deterrence, it will not reflect the nonviolence of Jesus. It will not uphold the Sermon on the Mount. It will continue to support the ultimate child abuse: the murder of children through warfare.

At the moment, most priests, bishops, and cardinals remain profoundly ignorant about the alternative of Gospel nonviolence and deeply naïve about our government, its wars, and their silence and complicity with injustice. In seminaries across the United States, the Scriptures are taught less and less, in favor of canon law, the catechism, and liturgical rules. It is as if we are no longer sleeping but have woken up and chosen, discipleship not to Jesus but to the law-abiding religious officials!

A False Spirituality of Violence

The Church still reflects the culture's false spirituality of violence, the belief that violence saves, that might makes right, that the good news is not "love your enemies" but "kill your enemies," that war is necessary, that war is justified, that war is even blessed by God. Over the centuries, the Church modeled itself on the empire, created a leadership system based on domination and "lording it over others," rejected the Sermon on the Mount as impractical, invented the just war theory, waged the Crusades, blessed nuclear weapons, and lived off the comforts of the culture of violence instead of risking the challenge of Gospel nonviolence, the cross, and the resurrection. Whenever churchmen support war, they not only support the way of empire but promote mortal sin.

There is no way to avoid the difficult, radical nonviolence of Christ. It is the center of his teachings. Until we embrace his nonviolence, we will continue to fall far short of his vision and follow the culture's false spirituality of war. But if the Church and all Christians adopt Christ's nonviolence, if we learn to love our enemies and resist our country's wars, we will not only find a new integrity and fidelity but may even stop the killing of children and the destruction of the planet itself. It is the job of all church leaders, pastors, ministers, and priests to speak publicly on behalf of the Gospel and the Christian community; denounce every war, bomb, and execution; and call everyone back to the wisdom of Gospel nonviolence.

In the end, the communities of faith, including the churches, the synagogues, and the mosques, will play a critical role in leading humankind back from the brink of destruction. The religious communities remain among the few civic groups who can stand with our country's enemies, see the humanity in their eyes, love them, and defend them. They still have the potential to denounce injustice, chastise war-making governments and presidents, and encourage public opinion into action for justice and peace.

As Martin Luther King, Jr., and the civil rights movement showed, the churches can play a key role in practicing active nonviolent resistance to systemic injustice and war, and in building the grassroots movement for social change. They can become prophetic communities that denounce war and injustice, and announce the vision of a more just, peaceful society, where war, poverty, and nuclear weapons no longer exist.

The Catholic Church must renounce once and for all its support of war. When the Church gives itself to the prophetic defense of all victims of war, and confronts the Pentagon and the government's wars, then it will discover true authenticity and resemble the radical vision of its founder. It will discover the power, integrity, and authenticity of the cross. It will finally wake up and witness the glory of the God of peace.

Dorothy Day fumed over the hypocrisy of Catholic priests, bishops, and cardinals. She lived among the homeless and spoke out vigorously for justice and peace, yet everywhere she faced opposition from male church leaders who lived in mansions and were driven in chauffeured limousines. "There are days," she once wrote, "when I want to stop all those poor people from giving their coins to the church, and tell them to march on the offices of the archdiocese, to tell all the people inside those offices to move out of their plush rooms and share the lives of the hungry and the hurt. Would Jesus let himself be driven in big black limousines, while thousands and thousands of people who believe in him and his church are at the edge of starvation, while people come to church barefooted and ragged and hungry and sick?" If we want to be authentic Christians, Day insisted, we must side with the poor, simplify our lifestyles, renounce our privilege, stand with our enemies, work for justice, and speak the truth of peace. Then our moral pronouncements will carry the weight of personal integrity and we might begin an authentic discipleship.

In particular, churchmen need to renounce sexism and

welcome women into leadership roles. Without the voice of women, we miss the potential for transfiguration from over half the human race. We lose the balance offered by feminine vision. With women in every ministry, we churchmen may finally learn to wake up.

We male church leaders have much to learn from women. They teach us what it means to be a church. They show us the church of the Transfiguration, the church of resurrection as a community of equality, justice, nonviolence, compassion, forgiveness, and peace. They teach us how to follow Jesus on the discipleship journey. Churchmen must awake from their slumber to the truth of gender equality and the call to unity.

If we priests and Christians were wide awake, vigilant, faithful, prayerful, and nonviolent, the Christian community would be transfigured. We would be filled with grace and come alive to God's disarming presence. We would oppose war and injustice, heal the broken, liberate the oppressed, make peace, and shine the light of God's presence everywhere. The world would be a better place because we would be doing our job: keeping watch with Jesus, accompanying him in his transfiguration, encouraging him on his journey, and loving him no matter what.

Awakening from Our Slumber

But we must go easy on the three male disciples. We all sleep through Christ's transfiguration. It is mighty hard to walk that long road with Jesus to Jerusalem; it is hard to climb a mountain to find God in contemplative solitude. We are tired from the journey. We are tired from the struggle. We are tired from the challenges, confrontations, and crises. We are tired from going against the grain. We are tired from the day-to-day rigor of family, work, travel, and routine. We are tired of war. We are tired of death. We are tired of the world itself. As Fannie Lou Hamer said, "I am sick and tired of being sick and tired." We too are overcome with sleep and cannot keep our eyes open, even as Jesus becomes the Light of God.

I know I would have collapsed on that mountaintop setting if I were one of those disciples. Like everyone, part of me is not yet awake to the presence of Christ and the call of the Gospel. Even the best people I know at times want to give up. There is nothing unusual in this somnolent discipleship; it was there from the beginning. Oddly enough, it offers us the hope that we too can wake up to the presence of Christ. If we can wake up, as Peter, James, and John eventually did, we may open our eyes to see the transfigured Jesus standing before us in all his glory.

As the Gospel reaches its tragic climax and astonishing denouement, Jesus tells his disciples—and all of us—that the time has come to wake up, keep watch, and get ready. "You know not the day or the hour!" Jesus says. He wants us to wake up from our long night's sleep and live fully alive for the rest of our lives.

_____

11

It Is Good for You to Be Here

W hen Peter, James, and John awake from their heavy sleep, they are scared out of their wits. There before them stand not only their rabbi Jesus in dazzling white light but the greatest religious heroes of their lives, Moses and Elijah, who had long since been dead. It is an apparition that thrills them with awe and wonder, one that would terrify any one of us today.

To make matters worse, as the disciples start listening to the conversation among Jesus, Moses, and Elijah, they realize that the saints are encouraging Jesus to go to Jerusalem, to speak out for justice and God, to risk his life, to accept the inevitable consequences of arrest and execution, and to understand his death as a gift for humanity, a new exodus from our slavery to violence and death.

The sleepy disciples, however, immediately start objecting to Jesus' plans and that spiritual conversation. They do what we all do: they cling to this spiritual experience of the Holy, reject its political and social ramifications, and try to institutionalize it. While their objections miss the entire point of the transfiguration story, they are nonetheless revealing and instructive. If we dare reflect on Peter's reaction, we might learn not to make the same mistakes Peter and the gang make.

Peter never encourages Jesus on his peacemaking journey, as Moses and Elijah do. Earlier, when Jesus announced that he would be arrested, tortured, and executed for disrupting religious and imperial business as usual in Jerusalem, Peter shouted out, "God forbid! That will never happen to you!" (Matt. 16:22). Upon awakening on the mountain, however, he blurts out: "Master, it is good for us to be here" (Matthew 17:4; Mark 9:5; Luke 9:33). In some ways, to put it bluntly, Peter does not really care about Jesus. He is not yet a true disciple, as the Gospels go out of their way to point out. He is not concerned with Jesus' needs, and he certainly does not support Jesus' mission. Rather, he wants to protect himself and make sure his own needs are met. He wants Jesus to be powerful and successful, and to use his own imperial authority to regain control for Israel. Peter asserts himself, tries to take control of the situation, and starts commanding Jesus, Moses, and Elijah to stay right where they are. In effect, he demands they stop all this talk about the cross, a new exodus, active nonviolence, and crucifixion.

Luke records Peter's words: "Master, it is good that we are here. Let us make three booths, one for you and one for Moses and one for Elijah." In other words, he says, "Forget the cross and suffering and death. Let's build some houses here on the mountain, a retreat center, and stay here forever, far away from Jerusalem and the Temple, far above the world and its political struggles, far away from any threat of crucifixion and death."

The Peter Within

The church activist Joan Chittister writes that Peter's declaration represents the classic struggle between false piety and true Christianity, "religion-for-real" and "religion-for-show." Here on the mountain, Peter tries to avoid the call to discipleship and the cross and, instead, claims a private piety, a new-age spirituality far removed from the messy, bloody struggle for justice and peace.

"Let's live in this nice, comfortable religious cloud," Peter says, in Chittister's translation.

> Let's institutionalize the mystical. Let's concentrate on the next world. Peter knows a good thing when he sees it and Peter plans to settle down in a nest of pieties and wait. At the very moment of his deepest revelation and clearest call, in other words, Peter decides that the spiritual life has something to do with building temples and keeping the rituals and enlarging the facilities and floating above the fray. If there is a temptation here, it is the temptation to play church, to dabble in religion, to recite the prayers without becoming them. But no sooner has Peter decided to be a church bureaucrat, a weekday mystic, an office manager, than the irony of the situation shocks us all: scripture dashes the entire thought in mid-air. (*National Catholic Reporter*, March 2, 2001)

As always, Peter and the disciples are self-centered, egotistic, and focused on what they want, not on what Jesus needs. If Peter truly cared about serving and following Jesus, he would say something entirely different. He would affirm Jesus, just as Moses and Elijah do. He would tell Jesus how good it is for Jesus to be there at this moment of consolation and confirmation by the holy ones. "How good it is for you to be here," he would say upon waking, putting the emphasis and focus on Jesus, his lord and master, instead of upon himself. Rather than pursuing his own agendas, Peter would rejoice that Jesus is getting such cosmic support before he embarks on the road to his execution. Peter would learn from Moses and Elijah to support Jesus from now on every step of the way.

For two thousand years, instead of affirming Jesus' way of the cross, the way of active nonviolence, and the struggle for justice and peace, the Church has preferred Peter's words. It has kept the focus on itself, its leaders, and its control over everyone else. Today, the best Scripture commentaries note how well Peter spoke, how good it was "for them to witness the glory of God." But like Peter, we have yet to support Jesus on the way of the cross. Rather, we have gone ahead and built thousands of sanctuaries, retreat centers, and mansions in which to stage our religious services, instead of sharing the suffering of the poor, speaking out for justice and peace, and risking our lives for nonviolent change.

In Mark, Peter address Jesus as "Rabbi." Luke's account uses the title "Master." Matthew's version records Peter saying, "Lord." In each case, Peter alludes to the Jewish Feast of Tabernacles, sometimes called the Feast of the Booths, or the Feast of Tents. The Feast of Booths originally celebrated the harvest (see Deuteronomy 16:13–17 and Leviticus 23:39–43). Worshipers built booths to symbolize the shelters of harvesters and to celebrate God's gift of the harvest. Each Gospel, especially John's (see 7:2–39), replaces these traditional Hebrew feasts with new Christian feasts, from baptism to Pentecost.

When Peter talks about building booths, he invokes the usual liturgical practices of his day. He calls for the institutionalization of the religious experience, with total disregard for the social and political implications of institutionalized religion. Jesus, by contrast, begins and ends his religious life by publicly confronting systemic injustice, religious hypocrisy, and imperial domination. He turns over the tables of the religious sanctuaries that operate at the expense of the poor and in collusion with the Roman military. His rejection of illegitimate religion and its complicity with injustice leads to his death. But Moses and Elijah help him realize again that the way of the cross, the way of suffering love, which insists on justice and nonviolence, is the ultimate, true, legitimate worship of God. Indeed, their presence affirms his path as authentic religious practice; it leads to mysticism, to the presence and glory of God.

Jesus maintains all along that authentic worship of the God of peace means we have to resist the empires of war and the systemic injustice that kills the world's poor. If one wants to be authentic before the God of love, one has to oppose institutionalized violence. This nonviolent resistance, the way of the cross, is the authentic spirituality of the Gospel. If we do not confront the systemic oppression of the poor and, instead, spend our lives supporting corporate greed, structured injustice, and institutionalized violence while going through the routine motions of obligatory worship, our religion is a waste of time. We are not practicing the Christianity described in the Gospels. For the Evangelists, authentic Gospel spirituality includes public confrontation with systemic injustice through creative nonviolence.

Peter's shock reflects the shock we all feel. Deep down, we know that Jesus is right and that the Gospel call to active nonviolence is the fullest expression of truth, integrity, and humanity. But who of us wants to go against the grain of popular culture? Who of us wants to rock the boat and speak out against the Pentagon and the flag? Who of us wants to be mocked, ridiculed, or harassed for our public disagreement with our government? Who of us wants to risk our lives by disrupting our government's wars and its corporate billionaires? Who of us wants to be so foolish as to take on the empire and its powers with our small, obscure, ignored acts of nonviolence?

There is a Peter lurking within each one of us. Like Peter, a major part of us is more concerned about protecting ourselves, boosting our egos, strengthening our security, and designing our own fate than about supporting Jesus as he goes to the cross. Like Peter, we prefer a comfortable mountaintop place where we can float above the fray, think pious thoughts, center ourselves in abstract spiritualities, keep God under control, and stay forever removed from our own explosive Jerusalems. Like Peter, we know that in faraway retreat centers we can delude ourselves into thinking that we are devout, religious, pious practitioners of authentic Christian worship. Like Peter, we tell ourselves that we are doing God's will and that "it is good for us to be here." Like Peter, we prefer to avoid the poor, the starving, the homeless, the sick, the imprisoned, the dying, the outcast, the marginalized, the troublemakers, and the victims of our wars. But like Peter too, we are going to have to learn that Jesus does not permit silence in the face of systemic injustice, that Jesus insists we speak out against idolatry and greed, that Jesus commands us to love our neighbors and our enemies, that Jesus takes up the cross of nonviolent resistance to war and calls every one of us to do the same.

As far as the religious expectations of the day are concerned, Peter's proposal is appropriate, even praiseworthy. He suggests a fitting religious response, what the most devout Pharisee or Sadducee might say. He responds to the apparition of the saints and the transfiguration of Jesus with a five-year plan, a capital campaign, contract negotiations, architectural plans, and the latest worship design. But in light of the conversation about the cross, Peter's proposal, like our own religious rituals, tries to control Jesus and God. Although his pious suggestion invokes the great religious feasts of his day, Peter tries to take charge of the situation, to protect Jesus, to contain the divine, to keep Jesus away from Jerusalem, to capture the glorified Jesus and the saints and put them under glass. Ultimately, of course, Peter is trying to protect himself from any threat of crucifixion. If he builds three booths, perhaps then Jesus and the saints will stay on the mountain and live happily ever after, without ever having to face the Roman Empire, the religious authorities, Herod, Pilate, or his cross.

A Jesus of Our Own Making

In a million ways, we all try to control God. If we could, we also would try to capture Jesus, keep him to ourselves, and pretend that we are living profoundly spiritual lives. For the pious and faithful, like Peter, our attempt at daily prayer is more often than not an exercise in telling God what to do. We tell God how good it is for us to be here with God, and we do everything we can to stay in that "good" place. We carry on the religious rituals that have gone on for centuries, while the nations of the world wage war after war, starve the poor, and mock the God of peace. While trying to keep Jesus to ourselves, we end up keeping everything to ourselves, instead of giving ourselves away. We do not stir up trouble, rock the boat, or make waves. We look the other way while the poor suffer and die under our bombs—all the while telling ourselves that we are doing God's will, meeting our religious obligations, and fulfilling our patriotic duty. In other words, we avoid the cross at all costs.

Jesus is entirely different from such patriotic, religious hypocrisy. He is a troublemaking revolutionary. He confronts injustice head-on and tells us that this is what religion is about. He teaches that loving the "wrong" people, resisting war, siding with one's enemies, and opposing unjust political leaders is the authentic way to God because, first of all, it is the authentic way to be human in inhuman times. It is the way to be with God because God sides with the poor, the marginalized, the oppressed, and the enemy.

Like the ancient prophets who condemned war and the religious rituals that blessed injustice, Jesus denounces our false piety and commands us to stop our wars, dismantle injustice, and feed the starving as the first step toward authentic religious practice. Because he practices what he preaches, he tells Peter he is going to Jerusalem to take nonviolent, direct action on behalf of justice and face the inevitable consequences.

Jesus cannot be controlled. Neither can God. God will not stay under our thumb. We can pretend to be as pious and spiritual as we want, but according to the Gospels, if we are not publicly, actively pursuing justice and peace, we are wasting our time. We are nowhere near the God of Jesus.

Peter's reaction to Jesus' contemplative nonviolence points
to the spiritual crisis that confronts us today. Instead of accompanying Jesus (and one another) on the way of nonviolent, suffering love, the way of the cross, we try to stop him and remain
on the comfortable mountaintop, far removed from Jerusalem.
Even with the beatific vision of Moses and Elijah, Peter tries to
dissuade Jesus from the cross. Peter insists that Jesus should listen to him. He thinks, as we all do, that he knows better than
Jesus.

If only Jesus would listen to us, we tell ourselves. Instead of
accompanying Jesus back down the mountain into the messy
confrontation with the authorities and its bloody outcome, we
resist Jesus. We refuse to listen to Jesus. We try to instruct Jesus.
Then, after every attempt at reforming Jesus and getting him to
conform fails, we give up, and like all the disciples, we walk
away from him, even run. Jesus is going to Jerusalem, where he
will confront the religious collusion with imperial injustice. The
ultimate choice before us, as Peter bitterly learned, is whether
or not we will accompany Jesus to his death and join him in the
nonviolent struggle for justice and peace.

When Peter proposed building three booths, the Evangelists
write, he did not know what he was saying. Likewise, today, as
we pray to God, gather in religious assembly, and fulfill our obligations for weekly worship, we do not know what we are saying. The Gospels record Jesus' journey to the cross and his
commandment that we put down the sword, but we focus on
religious ritual instead. We build bigger churches and our own
little religious empires. Instead of practicing the nonviolence of
Jesus, we create institutions, universities, retreat centers, super-
churches, fiefdoms, and nonprofit organizations where power,

profit, domination, and control remain the standard operating procedures. The cross is no longer a dangerous sign of our discipleship but a piece of art that symbolizes our control of God.

For centuries, the Church has tried to control God, to keep Jesus under wraps. Even though Jesus repeatedly challenged the religious authorities and practices of his day, any such challenge today results, as it did for Jesus, in marginalization if not excommunication. This ostracizing was the experience of Dorothy Day, Philip Berrigan, and the Salvadoran martyrs Rutilio Grande, Oscar Romero, and Ita Ford. Those church workers who advocate the ordination of women, the equality of all people, and nuclear disarmament, such as members of the lay movements Call to Action, the Catholic Worker, and Pax Christi, are pushed to the edge of the Church instead of brought into its center.

Like Peter, we prefer a messiah of our own making, one who stays put, who is passive, who listens to us, who does what we say, who remains aloof, who avoids politics, who does not rock the boat, who keeps our religious culture riding high, and who cooperates with our silent cooperation with systemic injustice and imperial militarism.

Like Peter, we do not know what we are saying or what we are doing. We think we are doing God's will, but most likely, we are merely doing our own will. The challenge is to shut up, stay focused on Jesus, accept what he says, do what he does, and follow in his footsteps.

Letting Go of Fear

Mark adds that Peter and the disciples did not know what to say to Jesus "because they were exceedingly afraid" (9:6). Why are Peter, James, and John exceedingly afraid? They are afraid of the apparition, the bright light, and the change in Jesus. They fear Moses and Elijah. Mostly, they are afraid of the conversation about the cross. They fear the political implications of this conversation for their own lives. What will it mean for them if Moses and Elijah are encouraging Jesus to go to Jerusalem and risk martyrdom for God's reign of justice? Will their popular healing ministry in Galilee be disrupted? If they have to leave this peaceful mountaintop, does that mean they have to give up their religious festivals and booths and risk martyrdom as well? Is martyrdom the goal of discipleship, the spiritual life, our own personal lives? Such questions frighten any of us.

Peter's fear challenges our own. What are we afraid of? Why are we afraid to love our enemies, speak out against injustice, go to our own Jerusalem, carry the cross, and risk our lives for justice? What drives us to control God, remain safe on contemplative mountaintops, build religious empires, and look the other way while millions die from our bombs and greed? What does authentic religion and true spirituality mean for us today? How do religion and spirituality connect to the struggle for justice and peace? These are scary questions, especially given the tumultuous headlines of our times. If our religious practice does not include pursuing nuclear disarmament, abolishing war, reconciling with our enemies, feeding the hungry, and dismantling injustice, then it does not fit into the conversation among Moses, Elijah, and the transfigured Jesus. If we dare engage the world in the spiritual, political transfiguring pursuit of justice and disarmament, then we too will have to face our fears.

Like Peter and the gang, deep down we are terrified. We are afraid of everything. We are afraid of snakes, spiders, mice, accidents, flying, bankruptcy, embarrassment, success, and failure.

We are afraid of one another. We are afraid of the police, our government, judges, intruders, outsiders, the enemy, and all those who are different from us. We are afraid of change, public attention, humiliation, pain, poverty, illness, arrest, imprisonment. We are afraid of heaven and hell. We are afraid of God, but most of all, we are afraid of death. This life of fear will literally be the death of us.

Gandhi said we can never begin the spiritual life of loving nonviolence until we conquer our fear of death. Once we let go of our fear of death, accept our deaths, and strive to live life to the fullest every moment, even to help end the onslaught of death that is war and injustice, we will be liberated. We can face anything. Like Jesus, Moses, and Elijah, we can turn to the cross, stand up for God's reign of life, and even risk martyrdom, the greatest love of all, by laying down our lives for suffering humanity.

The way of the cross is terrifying. Like Peter, none of us would knowingly and willingly lay down our lives for our friends, much less for the human race. In our country, few people attain such noble heights. Martin Luther King, Jr., and Malcolm X are shining exemplars. We have so repressed our fears that the cross is meaningless for all intents and purposes in day-to-day America. We go to our religious services on weekends and follow the political and military debates the rest of the week with passing interest or a sense of helplessness. We would rather watch football, go on vacation, sip our cocktails, stare at the television, or shop till we drop than encounter the transfigured Jesus. We pretend that we are not going to die, and any thought of death or any image of death or any invitation to death is dismissed out of hand. To hear the holy ones affirm Jesus' path of nonviolent resistance and its deadly outcome as the way of God throws our cultural assumptions out the window.

We live in fear and pretend we don't. Jesus, however, refuses to live in fear. He confronts fear head-on. He deals with it and moves beyond it. Moses and Elijah do the same. They do not let fear control their lives. Their transfigured glory is the fulfill-ment of lives that have overcome fear and reached the height of sacrificial love.

The more we enter into the mystery of Christ, the more we find ourselves "exceedingly afraid." Like Peter, we may start say-ing things even though we do not know what we are saying. But we have the example of Peter and his friends. We know ahead of time that we may be overcome with fear and start bab-bling in the presence of God. Knowing this possibility, we can prepare to respond with faith, hope, love, and trust.

If we can enter the presence of Jesus, recognize our fears, and give them to Jesus; if we can stop trying to control him and in-stitutionalize religious experience; if we can open ourselves to the mystery of God and the peace of Christ; if we can trust and accept God's unlimited, unconditional, forgiving love for each one of us and Jesus' personal concern for our well-being, then we will receive new grace to overcome fear and walk in peace. We will become like Moses and Elijah, faithful servants of the God of peace. We will see the light, enter God's glory, and know the meaning of Gospel transfiguration. We will be able to follow Jesus wherever he goes.

12.

This Is My Beloved

Just as Peter starts talking about building three tents where they could remain on the mountain forever, a bright cloud overshadows them and a voice speaks from the cloud saying, "This is my beloved Son. Listen to him" (Mark 9:7).

This moment is one of the most surprising, astonishing, and shocking scenes in the New Testament, if not in the entire Bible. God rarely speaks as dramatically as this to anybody, including Jesus. In the Hebrew Scriptures, we read how God speaks to Moses from a cloud on Mount Sinai. God's voice comes through this "cloud of unknowing" to instruct Moses to lead his people out of slavery into the promised land and to deliver the commandments of the new covenant. But suddenly, God speaks! God sides with Jesus! God encourages the disciples to follow this beloved Son to the cross in pursuit of God's reign of justice and peace.

The Evangelists evoke this image of God speaking to Moses through a cloud on Mount Sinai to heighten the drama of this peak experience in the life of Jesus and thus the entire human race. Once again, God is leading God's people out of slavery into liberation, and instructing the disciples on their new life by commanding them to listen to Jesus. Jesus is the Great Liberator, the new Moses, the Chosen One. From this "cloud of unknowing," God reveals Jesus' true identity as God's beloved Son to the disciples and instructs them to listen to him from now on.

God rarely speaks directly to Jesus like this, even in the Gospels. In fact, God never appears to Jesus. Only at his baptism does Jesus hear the voice of God naming him as God's beloved Son. Later, in the desert and in the Garden of Gethsemane, when Jesus resists the temptations to despair and doubt, angels will appear to console him. But only Luke records such a supernatural experience. The other three Gospels leave Jesus on his own, walking in blind faith and trust.

Here, at this critical moment in his life, Jesus and the disciples hear a voice coming from a cloud, affirming his life and thus confirming his mission, his upcoming pilgrimage to Jerusalem, and his public execution on the cross.

Each Evangelist, however, puts a slightly different twist on the moment. Luke writes that "a cloud came and overshadowed them; and they were afraid as they entered the cloud. And a voice came out of the cloud, saying, 'This is my Son, my Chosen; listen to him!' " (9:34–35). Matthew states that while Peter "was still speaking, a bright cloud overshadowed them, and a voice from the cloud said, 'This is my beloved Son, with whom I am well pleased; listen to him.' When the disciples heard this, they fell on their faces and were filled with fear" (17:5–6).

None of the Evangelists states flatly that this voice is the voice of God. Rather, they know that their readers will be familiar with the Exodus story, that they will immediately recognize the scene from that foundational moment when God spoke to Moses on Mount Sinai. They are confident their readers will conclude that the voice speaking from the cloud is none other than the voice of God. Readers know that this is God's way of communicating at pivotal moments in human history. God speaks through a cloud hovering over a mountaintop. They understand that the disciples, like Moses originally, are hearing the voice of the divine and being called, like Moses, to assist in God's liberation and transformation of humanity.

Jesus' Course Confirmed

The first word that God utters on Mount Tabor is to tell the disciples who Jesus is. God names Jesus as God's "beloved Son," "God's Chosen One." Jesus would already know this, so the message is clearly intended for his friends, for the Church, for us. But nonetheless, it must have been immensely consoling to Jesus. Once again, his core identity as God's beloved Son, the great news that he heard at the Jordan River after his baptism, is confirmed (Mark 3:21–22). With this second announcement and confirmation, Jesus must believe that his decision to go to Jerusalem and risk the cross is not only correct but divinely blessed. Much to the shock of Peter and the disciples, it is the will of God.

To understand God's declaration, we need to reflect on what happened by the Jordan River a few years earlier. According to Luke's account, Jesus had just been baptized by John the Baptist and was sitting by the river "praying" (3:21). We are presented with the scene of a contemplative, deep in meditation, a person attuned to the voice of God, someone who listens and waits for God to speak. Jesus was ready for that unknown moment when God suddenly spoke from the heavens. Perhaps he had been sitting in quiet prayer every day of his so-called hidden life. I presume that, like all of us, he was never quite sure what his vocation was. Like us, he did not know who he was or what his purpose on earth was. Until that moment, his life, like ours, was a mystery.

Then, suddenly, everything became clearer. The sky opened, and the Spirit of God descended upon him like a dove, and a voice came from heaven and said, "You are my beloved Son; with you I am well pleased" (Luke 3:22).

What a dramatic, life-changing moment! This was the greatest experience in the life of Jesus up until his transfiguration. This moment set the course for everything that followed, and changed human history.

I think Jesus spent the rest of his life living up to this magnificent calling. In that moment, he was set on fire by the love of God, whom he then called Abba, "Daddy." At that point, Jesus knew who he was. He accepted the declaration of the voice from the heavens, that he was the beloved of God and that his mission was to live as God's beloved Son, to do the will of his Abba. He decided there and then to be faithful to this identity as God's beloved, and indeed spent the remainder of his days fulfilling this vocation. Immediately after his baptism and the heavenly voice's declaration, the Spirit of God drove him into the desert, where he prayed and fasted for forty days, probably in an effort to sort out the meaning of this great message from the sky.

During that time in the wilderness, Jesus was tempted to reject the word from on high. How could he be the beloved Son of God? the demon said to him. At the beginning of each of the three temptations, according to Matthew and Luke, the demon said, "If you are the son of God," then prove it. Jesus was tempted to despair, doubt, dominate, and do violence to himself, but in each case, he rejected those temptations and clung to the word of love he had heard from God. He took God seriously and remained faithful to his identity. He chose to be the Chosen One. He accepted himself as God's beloved and decided to let the chips fall where they may. Whether or not humanity welcomed the gift of God's beloved Son, he would be who he was.

In the end, after a lifetime of rejection, when the authorities finally arrest and execute him, Jesus hangs on the cross in agony while the religious leaders, soldiers, and passersby mock him with the words of the tempter in the desert. "If you are the Son of God," they yell, "come down from the cross and prove it; then we will believe you." From the beginning of his public life to his bitter end, the question of Jesus' identity is crucial. Who Jesus is forms what he does and how people respond to him. If he is who he claims to be, the beloved of God according to the voice from heaven, then everything is changed; the empire no longer holds authority over humanity, the religious leaders have to let go of their hypocrisy and complicity with injustice, and everyone is summoned to hear and follow the Chosen One.

Humanity rejects Jesus' claim and its implications, and immediately crushes him. But to the bitter end, Jesus remains faithful to his core identity. He trusts his beloved God, and lives in faith and hope. He follows the meaning of his calling and acts always within the framework of his loving relationship with God. His last words then are an act of perfect surrender, love, and trust, based on that original voice from the heavens. "Into your hands, I commend my spirit," he says as he breathes his last.

What did it mean then for Jesus to be called by God "my beloved Son, my Chosen One"? This question is worth a lifetime of meditation. It is significant not only for our understanding of who Jesus is but also for our self-understanding and what it means to be his followers. In John's Gospel, we find Jesus over and over again imagining who he is. He tries to tell us who he is through a series of magnificent images: I am the Way, the Truth, and the Life. I am the gate. I am the Good Shepherd. I am the Light of the world. I am the Bread of Life. I am the Resurrection and the Life. I am the true vine. In the end, as the soldiers confront him in the Garden of Gethsemane, he utters the simple but loaded biblical words "I am."

After his baptism and desert fast, Jesus walks into Galilee and starts to announce God's reign of peace, to urge repentance from the culture of violence, and to teach God's way of love, most remarkably in his Sermon on the Mount. He is completely focused on and perfectly centered in God. He is fully present to God at all times, and thus fully present to himself and everyone around him. He possesses not a trace of the culture's violence, doubt, or despair, and so he is a perfect instrument of God's healing spirit of nonviolence. Even as the religious authorities reject his claim and his teachings, he remains steadfast and outspoken, calling for authentic worship of the God of peace, perfect compassion toward one another, and love for one's enemies.

The Gospel Course Rejected

Time and again, Jesus' message of nonviolence is rejected. Although he can see where all his actions are leading, to his final rejection and execution, he trusts the voice that named him "the beloved," and he lives out the implications of that belovedness, with almost ruthless disregard for the consequences.

What then does it mean for Jesus, at this moment of his transfiguration, to hear once again that voice from the heavens calling him "my beloved"? The voice of God does not terrify Jesus. It does not worry him. It does not make him anxious. Rather, the voice is immensely consoling and affirming. It is the only voice one would ever hope to hear, the one voice that Jesus trusts, the one voice that he constantly listens for and attends to. He stakes his life on the words of that voice and lives his life from the context of the voice that says, "I love you. With you I am well pleased!" In a life of constant rejection by family, friends, followers, and religious authorities, Jesus rarely hears words of affirmation and faith. These words from the Creator of the Universe, then, are the ultimate affirmation of love, and worthy of his life.

This announcement, however, comes at a particular juncture in his life, just after he tells his disciples that he must carry the cross, just after Moses and Elijah appear to encourage his upcoming execution as the ultimate "exodus" for humanity. The message from the cloud, then, is a divine sign of approval toward Jesus' ministry, teachings, public actions, and political confrontation in Jerusalem. Jesus has set himself on a mission of creative nonviolence in a desperately violent society, and God has now entered God's verdict on this path. God completely supports Jesus and his way of nonviolence. Jesus can trust that he is not just doing his own will but also responding to the will of the One who calls him "beloved."

The voice from the cloud, we can conclude, supports Jesus' way of loving nonviolence, active resistance to imperial injustice, and the way of the cross. God sees what Jesus is doing and where he is going. God tells the disciples in no uncertain words that Jesus is God's Chosen One, the Messiah, and, contrary to their hopes for a militant, violent, political revolutionary who will overthrow imperial injustice and establish a new kingdom of Israel, the God of the cloud sides with Jesus' version of messianic redemption. Jesus has declared himself a nonviolent messiah, the Suffering Servant of the prophet of Isaiah, who overcomes humanity's violence by resisting it through divine nonviolence, regardless of the capital crime and punishment that follow. God confirms that the Messiah is a nonviolent revolutionary, and that the path of suffering and martyrdom–not further violence and death–is the way to redeem and transform humanity.

On Mount Tabor, Jesus hears God tell his disciples that Jesus is God's Chosen One, which means that Jesus has been right all along. Thus, he will continue to trust completely in God's way of love and compassion, not in Peter's way, Pilate's way, Caesar's way, the Pharisees' way, or the empire's way. Jesus will carry on his campaign of revolutionary nonviolence, knowing that he is indeed fully loved by God, fully supported by God, fully blessed by God.

What must God feel, looking down on his transfigured beloved? The words portray God as a typical proud parent, unable to contain her pride and joy in her son, as if she wants to shout it from the mountaintop: "Isn't Jesus wonderful? What a terrific kid! He's the best son in the whole world!" But the words are serious. "This is my beloved Son. This is my Chosen One. This is the One with whom I am well pleased." In a culture that idolizes a firstborn son, the words paint God as a doting parent whose life revolves around the beloved son. For

Jesus, such a realization could only have brought consolation and joy.

Our Course Confirmed

As followers of the beloved Jesus, we have to ask ourselves: "What does Jesus' identity mean for me? How does it determine my identity? Who am I? What is my identity? What does God name me? What does Jesus name me?" Because we are Jesus' followers, our lives fit into his life. We share his journey, from his baptism through his active ministry and prophetic peacemaking to his cross and resurrection. That means that we find our identity in the life of Jesus, the beloved of God. Just as God calls Jesus God's beloved, so, with Jesus, God calls us God's beloved sons and daughters. We are Jesus' servants, friends, and disciples, and from the perspective of God, we are Jesus' sisters and brothers.

Our fundamental identity is found in Jesus and being named by God as God's very own beloved sons or daughters. This is a lifelong vocation and requires lifelong reflection and meditation. If we can embrace our identity with the same devotion Jesus did, we too will experience the height and depth and breadth of God's love.

Few of us actually grasp the truth of our identity as God's beloved, but nothing is more affirming, consoling, or liberating. To hear the voice of God call us God's beloved sons or daughters, we must take time, as Jesus did, to sit by the river in contemplative prayer, listening for God. This listening, of course, may take years, perhaps the rest of our lives. But one day, the heavens will open, and in our hearts we will hear God call us "my beloved." On that day, we will know the meaning of our existence. God has created every human being to be God's own beloved son and daughter. That means that the roughly 110 billion human beings who have ever lived were infinitely loved by God, that God considered each one individually as God's very own beloved son or daughter, and that God would go to any length to bring each one–including you and me–into God's house of peace.

If we can grasp the depth of this mystery, our lives will change for the better. Like Jesus, we will want to live every moment centered in this relationship of compassionate love with God. Everything we do will flow from the love we feel and hear from God. Every life decision we undertake will emerge from this loving relationship with God. Because we know God's boundless love for us, we will treat ourselves mercifully and nonviolently, loving ourselves in a healthy, wholesome way. Then, because we love ourselves and love our God, we will reach out with love, with hearts open toward the whole human race.

As Jesus explained in the Beatitudes, the sons and daughters of God become peacemakers. God is a God of peace, and God's children make peace with one another. To accept our calling as God's beloved sons and daughters means to become peacemakers. If we are God's beloved sons and daughters–and every human being is God's beloved son or daughter–then we are all, in the eyes of God, beloved sisters and brothers of one another. We must treat every other human being on the planet as our very own sister or brother. From now on, we understand that we are all equal, that we are already reconciled, that we are all united, that we are already one, that all life is sacred, that everyone is beloved by God, just as we are.

The social, political, economic, and human implications of

God's announcement are staggering. To be the beloved of God, for Jesus and each one of us, carries specific implications. Our common social belovedness requires us to practice nonviolence toward everyone on the planet. We can no longer hurt or kill or wage war against anyone, or allow others to suffer or starve or die, because every human being is our sister or brother, another beloved child of our beloved God. From now on, we are summoned to offer unconditional love and heartfelt compassion toward every human being. We have to resist poverty, violence, injustice, and war, and do everything we can not only to save the planet and the human race but to help one another discover our individual and collective calling to be the beloved children of God.

How do we begin such an enormous task? How can we ever fulfill our calling as God's beloved sons and daughters?

The voice from the cloud has one other message for us disciples. In this one command, we can find the answer to all our questions, problems, challenges, and vocation.

Listen to Jesus!

_____

13

Listen to Him!

<p>After the voice from the clouds announces "This is my beloved," it issues a specific order to the disciples: "Listen to him." God does not condemn, chastise, or hurt Peter and the other two disciples. Rather, God commands them to listen to Jesus. God wants them to pay attention to every word Jesus says and spend their lives acting on what they hear. Indeed, Jesus is the embodiment of the Word of God.

In this directive, we have one of the clearest and most neglected commandments of the Scriptures: Listen to Jesus. Here stands the great call of the Gospel, the divine way out of our personal problems and global nightmares, the way forward into a future of peace and justice, into God's reign. God is telling humanity, "Jesus is my beloved, the Faithful One, the Chosen One, the One who fulfills my every wish. Listen to him, be like him, speak like him, love like him, act like him." God repeats the words of Jesus' mother, Mary, to the waiters at the wedding feast in Cana: "Do whatever he tells you" (John 2:5).

A Life of Listening

What does it mean to listen to Jesus? What would it mean to take God seriously, to obey God's commandment, and to listen to Jesus conscientiously, deliberately, attentively for the rest of our lives? First of all, listening to Jesus means becoming people of contemplative prayer. Listeners are people who are quiet, at peace with themselves, attentive to others, fully present to God and humanity. If we dare listen to Jesus and do what he says, we need to take quality time every day to sit in silence and attend to his voice and his message. This may be difficult at first, but over time it can become the foundation of our day and lead not only to finding inner peace but to fulfilling the Word of God.

As we spend time each day in quiet contemplative prayer, we grow comfortable with silence and attentive to the voice within. If we are busy running around, pursuing our career ambitions, and racing to accomplish a million selfish errands, we will not be able to listen to Jesus. We will be oblivious to the voice of God. Listening to Jesus requires quality time, significant attention, serious dedication, and radical openness. It means moving beyond ourselves, the media, the nation, and the world and focusing on Jesus.

Second, to be listeners, we have to prepare ourselves to receive the Word, to let it settle in and take root in our hearts. As we become people of contemplative listening, we eventually notice every word that Jesus says, and we try to build our lives on his message, word by word, until we live and breathe his teachings. We focus ourselves with a single-minded devotion on his requests and their fulfillment in our own short lives. Then, with this single-minded devotion, we become what the New Testament calls "Keepers of the Word" and "Doers of the Word." If we listen to Jesus, our hearts melt and we fall in love with God. We become willing and able to accompany the transfigured Jesus wherever he goes, even down the mountaintop, to Jerusalem, to the cross and beyond.

Listening to Jesus requires familiarity with the four Gospels. If we want to know what he has to say, we need to know his story and read exactly what he is saying. It is helpful to read a few verses of the Gospels every day. We can study the text, mull over Jesus' actual words, contemplate the scene that Jesus finds himself in, and ponder what we would do if we were there with him. Then, we can try to apply his message, his text, and his story to our own concrete lives.

Third, listening to Jesus and doing what he says require consultation and conversation with other Christians. In addition to reading the Gospels every day, we need to discuss the text with friends and our local church community. We need to ask one another what we think Jesus means by these words, how we might translate his words into our current life and world situations, and then transform them into concrete action. In the midst of these spiritual conversations with other believers over the Word of God, we will begin to hear Jesus' word anew. His words come alive in community, and his Spirit moving among us will guide us to implement his words.

Finally, if we want to listen to Jesus, we need to hear his voice as he speaks in the world's poor, the enemy, the oppressed, the marginalized, the outcast, the imprisoned, and the dying. As Christians, we believe Jesus is risen and alive, active and at work among us. In fact, if we have ears to hear, we know that Jesus is speaking to us all the time. But we will not find his message on the front page of *The New York Times* or coming from the White House or the Pentagon. Jesus does not speak through the powerful, the rich, the warmakers, the nuclear weapons manufacturers, the president, the generals, the CIA director, the judges, or the police. Just as Jesus lived on the margins of his day, he continues to work on the margins today. If we want to listen to Jesus, we must be ready to hear him speak from the least likely place—which means we turn our attention to the disenfranchised, the oppressed, the victims, the starving, the bombed, and the enemy. We listen to the voice of the resisters, the peacemakers, those clamoring for justice, those demanding an end to war, poverty, and nuclear weapons. There we will hear the voice of Jesus speaking again.

Listening to the authentic voice of Jesus, then, requires choosing not to listen to other voices—the voices of the government or the media or the corporations or the warmakers or the nuclear weapons manufacturers. As disciples, from now on, we choose whom we are going to listen to.

The Voice of Jesus Speaking Today

It is not easy to listen to Jesus. Many people do not try; many give up. Listening to Jesus entails complete attention, full commitment, and steadfast devotion. We have to go to the fringe places, to the beat-up people, to the edge of the culture and the world. We have to struggle to hear his voice and determine that we will do what he says, even if we do not fully understand it.

Where is Jesus speaking today? If we listen closely, we can hear Jesus:

- in the world's poor and marginalized who suffer and die because of systemic global injustice, because of the unjust hoarding of the world's resources by the handful of richer nations
- in the starving masses, the 850 million people who are currently malnourished, who cry out for bread and water
- in the imprisoned, the tortured, the homeless, the ill, the lonely, the tormented, the dying
- in the laughter, longings, and tears of the world's children looking to us for peace
- in the pleas of our enemies, who long to be loved by us, to live life in peace
- in the world's war zones, from Baghdad to Gaza, from Kabul to Jenin, from Managua to San Salvador, from Port-au-Prince to Bogotá, from Bosnia to Rwanda
- in the dead of Iraq, Afghanistan, Palestine, Rwanda, Bosnia, Israel, Sudan, Central America, Southern Africa, Northern Ireland, and our own city streets, who cry out, "Stop the killing, stop the bombings, stop the violence"
- in the silence of the ashes of Hiroshima and Nagasaki
- in the voices of the Hibakusha, the atomic bomb survivors, who call for total nuclear disarmament and the abolition of war
- in the voices from death row who call for the abolition of the death penalty
- in the tens of millions who suffer and die from HIV and AIDS because U.S. pharmaceuticals companies will not freely release available drugs and the United States will not commit itself to eradicating this disease
- in all those who differ from us; in human variety with no regard for race, creed, nationality, gender, class, orienta-

tion, ability, or age; in the stranger at our door; in the vision of a forgiven, reconciled humanity

- in the faithful women of the world, who, unlike the somnolent male disciples, remain wide awake, announcing a paradigmatic shift, the fall of patriarchy and the birth of a just Church and a new society based on equality, dignity, and respect
- in the solitude of creation, from the mountaintops to the oceans to the desert, in the gentle rain and silent breeze, in the animals and birds, the fish and the insects—all praising the Creator, the God of Life, the God of Peace
- in our own hearts, in our own breath, in our own prayer, telling us how much God loves us all, that we too are God's beloved sons and daughters, invited to be transfigured in love so that we can follow Jesus down the mountain to the nonviolent cross in a spirit of love

"Listen to him!" the voice from the clouds says. One would think that the booming voice from the clouds would be egocentric, like us, shouting out, "Listen to *me*!" Instead, the modest, humble God calls attention not to himself but to his beloved Son. God imitates John the Baptist, who pointed to Jesus and said, "Behold the Lamb of God. He must increase." If we want to deepen our spiritual life, the message is clear: all we have to do is listen to Jesus.

What Jesus Is Saying

With the awesome voice of God urging us to turn our attention from the overshadowing cloud to the transfigured Jesus, we ask ourselves, "Well, what exactly is Jesus saying?"

As I read the Gospels, I discover a few essential teachings that make up the core of Jesus' message. These essential teachings are hard sayings, but they are the words we are commanded to hear, the words Jesus speaks when we try to listen. We could call them "Jesus' Greatest Sayings." These essential Gospel statements are enough to guide us for life. Not only do we find in them a specific path but we hear in them a way out of the world's madness. These quintessential sayings of Jesus are what the voice in the cloud is asking us to hear—and do:

1. Love your enemies, and pray for those who persecute you, that you may be sons and daughters of God (Matthew 5:44; Luke 6:27–28).
2. Love one another as I have loved you (John 13:34).
3. Repent, for the reign of God is at hand (Matthew 4:17).
4. Forgive and you will be forgiven (Luke 6:37).
5. Be compassionate just as God is compassionate (Luke 6:36).
6. The Spirit of the Lord is upon me because he has anointed me to bring good news to the poor (Luke 4:18).
7. Seek first God's reign and God's justice and all these things will be given you besides (Matthew 6:33; Luke 12:31).
8. Blessed are you who are poor, for the reign of God is yours (Luke 6:20).
9. Blessed are those who hunger and thirst for justice, for they will be satisfied (Matthew 5:6).
10. Blessed are the peacemakers, for they will be called sons and daughters of God (Matthew 5:9).

11. Do not offer violent resistance to one who does evil (Matthew 5:39).

12. You cannot serve God and money (Matthew 6:24).

13. Let the one who is without sin be the first to throw a stone at her (John 8:7).

14. Do not be afraid (Matthew 10:31, 14:27, 28:10; Mark 5:36, 6:50; Luke 8:50, 12:7, 12:32; John 6:20).

15. Go and learn the meaning of the words, "I desire mercy, not sacrifice" (Matthew 9:13).

16. Do unto others what you would have them do unto you (Matthew 7:12).

17. Those who live by the sword will die by the sword (Matthew 26:52).

18. As you enter a house, wish it peace (Matthew 10:12; Luke 10:5).

19. Behold, I am sending you like sheep in the midst of wolves (Matthew 10:16).

20. Whatever you did for one of these least sisters or brothers of mine, you did for me (Matthew 25:40).

21. Whoever wishes to come after me must deny himself, take up his cross, and follow me. What does it profit to gain the whole world and lose your soul? (Matthew 16:24, 26; Mark 8:34, 36; Luke 9:23, 25).

22. Whoever wishes to be great among you shall be your servant; whoever wishes to be first among you shall be your slave (Matthew 20:26–27; Mark 10:43–44).

23. Put your sword back (Matthew 26:52; John 18:11).

24. Follow me (Matthew 9:9; Mark 2:14; Luke 5:27; John 21:19).

25. Peace be with you (Luke 24:36; John 20:19, 21, 26).

These words from God's beloved Son have the power to transfigure our lives and the world. There are many other messages from Jesus, but if every Christian put all her or his energy into listening to and obeying these specific, hard sayings, the world would be transformed. The killing, starvation, and war-making would stop. We would discover the will of God and what it means to be children of God. These wise words show us how to be human, how to live, how to love, and how to dwell in peace. They open the door to wisdom, the spiritual life, and the fullness of life itself.

But these sayings are not about a private, Sunday morning piety. Jesus does not command obedience to any religious officials, duties, or rituals. Rather, he offers a definite social, economic, and political agenda. He speaks about active nonviolence, unconditional love, perfect compassion, justice for the poor, and persistent reconciliation toward every human being, regardless of class, gender, race, nationality, creed, or any other category. Surprisingly, the total message is focused not on God but on a new ethics, the values of nonviolent behavior toward other human beings, including entire nations. If we listen to Jesus, we learn to listen to and love one another and see him in everyone.

Why We Don't Listen

Why does God tell us to listen to Jesus? Because we do not listen to him. From God's perspective, Jesus is the only faithful human being. God knows we need to listen to Jesus, and God sees that we do not want to listen to him. God's commandment leads us to confess: we have not listened to Jesus, nor do we want to listen.

Why? Why do we not want to listen to Jesus? Why do we resist hearing what Jesus says? We do not listen to Jesus because we want to be in control. We want to remain in charge of our lives. We want to be God. We are afraid of the unknown. We do not want to be admonished or corrected. We know in our hearts that most of our behavior, especially our treatment of the poor and our enemies, is "an abomination in the sight of God," as Matthew's Gospel puts it. We know that Jesus will tell us to do what we do not want to do, to go where we do not want to go, to say the words that we do not want to say, and to live the way we do not want to live. We know that Jesus will call us beyond our narrow perspective, to the larger vision of God, which embraces the whole human race.

Instead of listening to Jesus, we prefer to do the talking. We want Jesus to listen to us. We want to tell him what we want him to do. If he would only listen to us, we tell ourselves, he would not advocate love for one's enemies. He would encourage us to make money, get ahead, be successful, look out for ourselves, forget the poor, hate one another, reject the marginalized, support the empire, take up the sword, and build more nuclear weapons. He would reject the cross and join us in our pursuit of global domination, even in the regrettable but necessary crucifixion of the world's poor.

But God overshadows the disciples and all of us, and declares in no uncertain terms: "Listen to him!" If we dare set aside our fears and give Jesus a chance, we may find that his words are healing, peacemaking, and life-giving. Indeed, we will discover to our shock and surprise that Jesus knows better than we do what we need. He knows us better than we know ourselves. His words actually have the power to make us better individually, communally, nationally, and globally.

The Wisdom of Listening

"Come to me, listen, and you will live," God says, according to the prophet Isaiah (55:3). "Everyone who belongs to the truth listens to my voice," Jesus tells Pilate, just before Pilate orders Jesus' execution (John 18:37). Pilate has no idea what Jesus is talking about. "What is truth?" he asks—but he does not wait to listen. Yet those who seek the truth and love the truth wholeheartedly listen to God and listen to Jesus.

The great figures of our times were first and foremost people who listened to the voice of God and the voice of Jesus. Mohandas Gandhi, Edith Stein, Thomas Merton, and Oscar Romero were contemplatives, prayerful people who rearranged their lives so that they could hear the Word of God and do what that Word said. Because they listened to God's word, heard God's word, took God's word seriously and responded to God's word with concrete action, they spoke God's word to God's people. They became prophets of peace and justice to a world of war and injustice. They made the world a better place. Their lives bore good fruit.

Toward the end of her life, Dorothy Day of the Catholic Worker movement reflected back on the days before her conversion, when she was an atheist and anarchist:

> I don't look back with regret. They were fine people. Their hearts were in the right place and their minds awake. But what we were doing—that was what we believed in; and so we were almost completely centered on techniques and strategies. . . . Today, I have a different perspective of why I am here on this earth and what I should do, and that's why I encourage all of us to make

God a part of what we do, to bring God into the midst of our decision-making.... That is why I am always mindful of prayer when we talk and hope and plan and worry.... So I listen, and I go to church, and I remember what I've heard, and I think of Jesus, and how he lived his life, and what he told the people he met, and I sit there and then it wells up in me, a notion of what should happen. (Robert Coles, *Lives of Moral Leadership* [New York: Random House, 2000], 149–50)

Dorothy Day and all the great Christians and peacemakers of our time listened first and foremost to God, to Jesus, and then they responded to what they heard. That is what we have to do. That is what God asks of all of us.

Prophets are people who announce God's word to the world. But to speak God's word, prophets first must hear that word from God, from Jesus. They attend to every word that comes from the mouth of God, dedicate their lives to God's message, and then spend their days putting that word into practice and announcing it. The same is true for each of us. If we dare listen to the voice of Jesus, we will hear the good news of peace and receive it as a gift. And then, announce it to the world.

When we attend to the voice of Jesus and meditate on his word, we are transfigured. If we obey his command, our hearts are disarmed of inner violence. If we do what he says, we will put down our swords and renounce our violence. We will beat our swords into plowshares, love our enemies, and pledge never to study war again. We will join the campaign to dismantle every nuclear and conventional weapon of mass destruction, spend our resources alleviating human suffering, and heal the earth. We will witness to the nonviolent reign of God in our midst. We will become people of contemplative nonviolence in a world of violence and, like Jesus, be people who listen to God.

When we listen to Jesus' voice, we discover a new vision for ourselves and the human race, and find the desire to walk with Jesus down the mountain into the world wherever he may lead us.

14

Rise and Do Not Be Afraid

G od is the only comfort," C. S. Lewis wrote. "God is also the supreme terror, the thing we most need and the thing we most want to hide from. God is our only ally and we have made ourselves God's enemies. Some people talk as if meeting the gaze of Absolute Goodness would be fun. They need to think again."

When the cloud overshadows the disciples and a voice speaks, they are terrified. This is understandable, and worth our reflection.

The three versions of our story offer slightly different variations. In Mark's account, the disciples wake up, see Jesus transfigured into white light with Moses and Elijah, and become afraid. Peter speaks about building three tents, we are told, because "he hardly knew what to say, they were so terrified" (9:6). Luke describes the coming of the cloud as the reason for their fear. "While Peter was still speaking, a cloud came and cast a shadow over them, and they became frightened when they entered the cloud" (9:34). According to Matthew, the disciples are terrified because of the voice, which tells them to listen to Jesus. "When the disciples heard this, they fell prostrate and were very much afraid. But Jesus came and touched them, saying, 'Rise, and do not be afraid.' And when the disciples raised their eyes, they saw no one else but Jesus alone" (17:6–8).

Why are the disciples afraid? In Mark, they fear the vision of God, the transfigured Jesus, and the saints with him. In Luke, they fear the presence of God in the cloud. In Matthew, they fear the voice of God commanding them to listen, because they do not know where the voice comes from, nor do they want to listen because they are afraid of what they might be told.

The Lies of Fear

Fear runs through each account of the transfiguration story. All of these fears reflect our own fears. Any of us would be afraid if we were there on that mountaintop. The Evangelists are telling us something about the human encounter with God, the mission of Jesus, and our fearful response. In other words, the Gospels ask, "What are we afraid of?"

In New York City, in the days after the destruction of the World Trade Center and the anthrax attacks, we were afraid. We could see fear in everyone's eyes, not knowing if there would be more terrorist strikes. We did not know if more planes would be hijacked, more buildings bombed, more people killed. These violent attacks filled us with fear, just as our violent attacks on Afghanistan, Iraq, and Colombia terrify millions of people around the globe. War instills fear.

We are living in a time of great fear. Most of us are terribly afraid. If we say we are not afraid, we are probably working overtime to distract ourselves from the fear that lies just below the surface of our awareness. We engage in endless activity, work overtime, sit for long hours in front of the television, eat too much, drink too much, and do whatever helps us avoid reality. But deep down, we are afraid. We do not tell one another that we are afraid. We do not try to help one another not be afraid—because no one teaches us how not to fear. On the contrary, the government and its war-making institutions try to keep us afraid, so that we will not be fearless and then try to stop the government's wars. Fear is one of the great tools of war-making culture. When we are afraid, we stay home, mind our own business, and leave the government to get on with the business of war. "Be afraid," the culture of war says. "Be very afraid." And we listen; we listen to the lies of fear.

Many things make us afraid. We fear loneliness, rejection, sickness, poverty, insecurity, pain, accidents, getting old, and facing loss. Most of all, we fear dying and death. Our culture practices massive denial about the truth of death. In fact, we have been socialized into avoiding the reality of death, the truth that someday, no matter how hard we try to avoid it, we will die. As the Tibetan Buddhist nun Pema Chödrön writes, it is the one undeniable fact of life, that each one of us will die, and every one of us, every day of our lives, acts as if this were not true.

Part of our resistance to death and dying lies with a culture that believes it will live forever. America is all about youth, success, power, celebrities, being number one, never getting old, never dying, always being on top, ruling the world. We have adopted the philosophy of the Nazis, though no one would ever put it that crudely. America thinks it will live a thousand years, like a new "1,000-Year Reich." For a culture that denies death and prizes life, America is ironically obsessed with death and doing the works of death, by systemically killing people through warfare, building new nuclear weapons, and ignoring human suffering. Most of us act as if we were not the most deadly people who ever lived—yet we are. Any attempt at questioning this culture of death immediately draws suspicion and condemnation, sometimes even prison and death.

We have so deeply integrated fear into ourselves that we can no longer think straight or act lovingly. We are numb to the business of death and live as if we were never going to die. Yet, despite what our culture tells us, at some point each one of us will die. When we do, the culture will turn away from us. There will be no grieving, no acknowledgment, no love for life.

One hundred twenty-five years from now, every human being alive at the moment I write this sentence—including you and me—will be dead. We will not exist in our physical bodies. My family and friends and all the people I have met and loved over the years will be dead. Our rulers, presidents, celebrities, popes, and bishops will be dead. The generals, bombers, torturers, FBI agents, CIA spies, School of the Americas soldiers, judges, TV anchors, congressional representatives, Pentagon officials, Trident submarine officers, nuclear weapons manufacturers: all will be dead. The billions of poor people around the world who suffer like Lazarus at the gate of Dives will also be dead. Where will we be? What will happen to us? What will we be doing? What will God say to us? How will we relate to one another then?

The Truth of Reality

The mysteries of life, death, and fear demand daily meditation if we are to grasp the truth of reality, the meaning of life.

The fruit of our meditation will summon us to prepare ourselves for our eventual death, not only so that we die well but
so that we live well and love well. Prayerful reflection about our
fears and our death can lead us to understand anew how precious life is, to use our time more wisely, to try to help others,
to live each moment in peace, and to grow in compassionate
solidarity with the whole human race. In other words, a meditation on death will lead us to God and what it means to be
human. It will help us to break through our denial and the culture of death, so that we can confidently confront our fear of
death and face the reality of life after death in God's house of
peace.

If we live in fear and succumb to the numbness inspired by
the culture, we will not be able to go deeper into the meaning
of life and the way of compassionate love. The more we let fear
rule our lives, the more trapped we will be, because fear prevents us from living and loving. It stops us from opening our
hearts to the truth of reality, seeing the transfigured Christ in
our midst, listening to him, and following him.

Jesus does not live in fear. Rather, he confronts fear head-on,
perhaps as the most fearless person who ever lived. There is no
room for fear in Jesus because he lives with a passionate love for
God and for every human being on earth. He lives in the present moment, fully awake, aware of his intimate relationship
with his beloved God. He is firmly rooted in faith, hope, and
love. This trust in God and the compassionate love Jesus feels
toward everyone dismisses his fears and leads him to work miracles everywhere he goes. No one had ever seen such fearless
love in action.

Because he is fearless, Jesus is not possessed by death. It is
not that he denies death. Rather, he is fully aware of it. He un-

derstands the meaning of death and sees beyond to God, judgment, the reign of heaven, and the fullness of life. Because he lives in the truth of reality, he sees the big picture far ahead, into the new life of resurrection. Because he is so full of life, Jesus does not inflict death on anyone. He cannot—because he is also free from the vestiges of death, including resentment, revenge, and retaliation. Jesus will not kill anyone or support the killing of any human being in history, no matter how justified the cause may appear to us, because he does not have a trace of death lurking within him. He is free from death. He is well beyond fear, focused on God, and so he willingly confronts death and risks resurrection. And, as we see in the life of Jesus, the only response that the culture of death knows to someone so free from death is to kill him.

Jesus stakes his life on his intimate relationship with his beloved God, so there is nothing left to fear. He does not fear any human being, or what any human being can do to him. He knows that his survival is guaranteed, that the least others can do to him is kill him, and that he will live in eternity with his beloved God. Jesus lives in the freedom of God's love, in the hope of resurrection, in the peace of the present moment, where there is nothing to fear.

If we confront our fears head-on, like Jesus, we too can learn to live without fear, to be centered in peace. "The opposite of love is not hate," I once heard Henri Nouwen say, "it's fear." Perfect love casts out all fear, the New Testament teaches. If we can love everyone around us and even love our enemies, we will not live in fear. We will be in love with everyone, including our enemies and God, and in that loving, we will find peace. We will recognize and acknowledge our fears, but we will not give them the power to control our lives. Rather, we will place our trust in the God of peace and the transfigured Jesus. We will try to grow in awareness of God in the present moment, and there, now, in that peace, we will try to breathe in the Holy Spirit of peace and breathe out our fear and lack of faith.

Moving Toward Fearlessness

If we take God at God's word, listen to Jesus, and try not to be afraid, after a while we will find that, in fact, our fears slowly evaporate, or at least take a backseat. Even as we face reality, including the reality of our personal deaths, fear will not govern our lives. We will grow in contemplative mindfulness, breathe in the peace of the present moment, love everyone with a wide, generous, compassionate spirit, and receive the grace of fearlessness. We will return to God's immeasurable, personal love for us, and to Jesus, who invites us into his friendship, his life of peace.

With time, as we remain centered in prayerful peace, we will become more and more alive. We will wake up to the present moment and show compassion to those around us. We will surrender ourselves to God, accept God's gift of peace to us, dwell more and more in God's reign, speak out against the culture's wars, even let go of our lives, welcome death, and anticipate the new life of resurrection in God's home. In other words, as we let go of fear, we become freer.

We were not created to live in fear. Rather, we were created to live in peace and love with ourselves, with one another, with the whole human race, and with God. If we believe in God, look for God, listen for God, listen to Jesus, and stay centered in Jesus' presence, we will no longer be terrified. We will not have time or energy to be afraid because we will be so focused on Jesus. This will not happen overnight, however, and it will not come easily. There is no quick ride to fearlessness. It is a lifetime journey that requires discipline, community, prayer, simplified lifestyle, selfless love, and a compassionate heart toward one's self and humanity. Over time, the Scriptures and the saints promise, we can grow into fearlessness.

Mahatma Gandhi worked at fearlessness every day of his life. As a boy, he lived in fear. He was terrorized by the darkness of the night. When he became a lawyer, he was so afraid, he could not speak in public. In fact, during his first court appearance, he became so paralyzed with fear that he could not open his mouth. He left the room ashamed and embarrassed as his colleagues laughed at him. Early on, he realized that if he was to engage in public work against racism and segregation in South Africa through active, nonviolent resistance, he would have to overcome his fears. He discovered that nonviolence requires fearlessness. Eventually, when he professed vows of nonviolence, poverty, truth, and chastity to formalize his commitment to God and God's way of peace, he also professed a vow of fearlessness. For the rest of his life, over forty years, he prayed every morning to live free from fear. "I will fear no one today," he prayed each morning. "I will not live in fear. I will fear only God, and so I will love everyone and seek God in everyone." Because he was so free from fear, he stood up publicly, called for India's independence from Britain, suffered six years in prison, faced countless failures and death threats, and anticipated his assassination with equanimity, prayer, and forgiving love for his assassin. Fearlessness made all the difference. Gandhi learned to live in faith, hope, and love—and his effort helped change the world.

The disciples are afraid when Jesus is transfigured, when the cloud overshadows them, and when the voice speaks from the cloud. Even when the voice speaks gentle words of invitation, the disciples become all the more terrified. They eventually stand up because Jesus calls them to rise above their fears.

The Call to Resurrection

Just at this moment, according to Matthew's Gospel, Jesus takes action and speaks to the disciples. It is the only line that Jesus speaks during the transfiguration experience. After the voice speaks from the clouds, according to Matthew, the transfigured Jesus bends down to the terrified disciples, who lie on the ground in front of him as if they are dead. He touches them and says, "Rise, and do not be afraid!" (17:4). When they look up, they see only Jesus.

Rise and do not be afraid! Here we have a new commandment, a way out of all our problems, our fears, and the culture of death itself—a way into the peace and new life of discipleship to Jesus.

When we are most afraid, Jesus reaches out, touches us, and calls us to the new life of resurrection. His outstretched hand, his saving touch, his kindness is the way out from under all that terrifies us, that scares us to death, that keeps us dead. He speaks healing, liberating words: "Rise, and do not be afraid." In our culture of fear and death, Jesus' invitation is good news. "Stand up," he says. "Be resurrected. Come alive and do not be terrified."

First, we notice that we are just like the disciples, lying prostrate on the ground, as if we are dead. Although we go through the motions of life, a large part of us is, in fact, dead. We are victims of the culture of fear and death, and most of the time, we do not even know it. Instead of living, we go on dying. Instead of following Jesus on the path to life, we prefer our daily grind, our meaningless jobs, our pursuit of riches, and our functional despair. Instead of rising with Christ, we prefer our culture of killing and living off the benefits of First World greed. We are quite content with the culture of fear and death, though we are clueless about the spiritual consequences of our indifference, our idolatry, our faithlessness, and our lack of love.

But as we lie facedown, dead, without even knowing it, the transfigured Jesus touches us and speaks to us, saying, "Rise! Live! You are no longer dead! You do not have to be victims of the culture of fear and war any longer. You no longer need to wallow in despair. You do not have to be dead any longer. You do not have to lie facedown, helpless, oppressed, terrified anymore. I am raising you up! You who were dead, now live! Get up! Live and let live! Live life to the full! Be risen, be transfigured, be the beloved with me! Live my life of love and peace!"

The transfigured, glorified Jesus commands us to live as resurrected people. He summons us to enter the glorious transfiguration of his resurrection. He calls us to share what he is going through and to taste the fullness of new life in God's reign of peace. Even though we may prefer to be dead, to go along with the culture of death, to be good, all-American citizens who pay taxes for war and nuclear weapons, Jesus tells us to rise. He says it is time to get up and not be dead anymore. And because he wants us to live, he will not let us die. He will not allow fear and death to rule us. He will not let the culture of death push us down into fear and despair. "I have come that you may have life and life to the full," he says in John's Gospel (10:10). In the face of fear, despair, and death, the fearless, transfigured Jesus who faces his own death, who believes in his beloved God, and who trusts his own resurrection tells us to rise up and live as he does. We are freed from fear, despair, and the culture of death. Jesus wants us to face our own deaths, believe in our beloved God, and trust in our own resurrections.

If all Christians took this commandment seriously, our lives would change for the better, as would our world. We would not give in to despair. We would not remain helpless or indifferent in the face of injustice. We would not support the culture of death. Rather, we would reach out in love and compassion toward others, especially the poor and the enemy. We would resist the infliction of death on other people. We would intervene with all war-making and say, "No more killing! We are not participating in death anymore. We are people of life."

To be people who "rise" means to be people who are fully alive, free from the culture of death, free even to speak out against the culture's love of death. From now on, we face death squarely and say with the risen Jesus, "No more death! We are a risen people, followers of the transfigured Jesus. We will not cooperate with the culture of war. We will resist war and killing from now on, for the rest of our lives, even to the point of death. You can persecute us, mock us, harass us, punish us, imprison us, even kill us, but from now on, we will not cooperate with the big business of death. We are risen. Until our dying breath, we say, 'In the name of the risen Jesus, stop the killing!' "

To live out this new commandment means to become people of the resurrection. But to risk the resurrection of our own lives means to accept the social and political implications of resurrection. The more we contemplate the meaning of Jesus' resurrection and his command to rise, the more horrified and terrified we will become! Rising up means standing up, speaking out, and opposing the culture's love of death. It means risking our lives just as Jesus did. It means confronting all those political, military, and economic systems that are anti-resurrection, all those institutions dedicated to weapons of mass destruction and the murder of the poor. It means becoming antiwar activists and peacemakers.

Resisting war is a scary task; people will get upset. People will defend their right to kill for whatever reason, even in the name of the nonviolent Jesus. Why do they support the culture's wars and injustice? Because they are scared. Because they have lost faith in the God of peace. Because they do not want to rise. Neither do we. All of us prefer the culture of war and injustice. We have grown comfortable with our First World reality. We like our presidents and generals, we idolize our celebrities and millionaires, we trust the media's version of reality, their commitment to capitalism, militarism, and classism. We have placed our security in our government, its weapons, its version of the truth, its power, its bombs. We know that if we dare resist the war-making government, we will be ostracized and ridiculed by family and friends, perhaps even hauled into court or thrown into jail. We know that if we follow the teachings of Jesus all the way, some of us, like Martin Luther King, Jr., and Oscar Romero, might even be arrested and killed.

Rise and be not afraid? Are you kidding? We want to stay dead and be very, very afraid. At least, that is something we are familiar with.

But Jesus changes everything. He reverses Dante and says, "Take on hope, all ye who enter here! Have hope, trust in me, you will live!"

"Do Not Be Afraid"

One reaction to this commandment and, later, to the actual resurrection of Jesus is sheer terror. There is nothing scarier than transfigured beings, risen martyrs, inviting us to follow them, to do what they did, to say the things they said, and to risk martyrdom. That is why the commandment "Rise" is followed immediately by the commandment "Do not be afraid." Jesus does not want us to live in fear.

Fearlessness and resurrection are intimately linked. The new life of peace and nonviolence that Jesus lived and to which he summons us requires fearlessness. God did not create us to live in fear. Rather, God invites us to live in compassionate, nonviolent love with and for one another. If we are going to rise up and live to the fullest, we cannot live in fear. The two simply cannot go together. The risen life is a life of fearless love, hope, and peace. "From now on," Jesus says, "I want you to live in peace and love with everyone, just as I do. That is the fullness of life—and that is my desire for you, my beloved. Do not despair. Live in hope of dwelling with me and my friends in peace forever."

If Jesus is clear about anything, it is his insistence that we are not to live in fear. The commandment "Do not be afraid" appears exactly 365 times in the Bible, more than any other commandment of God. Likewise, the one message Jesus says to his terrified disciples over and over again, more than any other saying in all four Gospels, is "Do not be afraid." (See Matthew 10:31, 14:27, 28:10; Mark 5:36, 6:50; Luke 8:50, 12:7, 12:32; John 6:20.) Jesus knows how terrified we are, and he has compassion on us. That is why he touches us. He is gentle and kind. He give us the best wisdom he has: "Rise, and do not be afraid."

With his touch, his word, his example, and his love, he gives us the faith and the strength to stand and live.

When the disciples open their eyes, they find themselves looking into the eyes of Jesus. There he is, standing alone, his usual, welcoming self. If we listen to Jesus and rise and refuse to live in fear, we too will open our eyes and find ourselves standing before Jesus. Our fears will vanish. All that terrorizes us will evaporate. We will find new strength, new grace, new hope, and new faith to follow Jesus wherever he goes. We will start acting like Jesus, as if we are already risen and have nothing to fear.

Just at that moment, Jesus will start the journey back down the mountain on the road to Jerusalem.

QUESTIONS FOR REFLECTION

1. When have you felt the presence of God in your life, moving in you, touching you, acting in your life and the world?

2. How do you move from the world's darkness into the light of Christ, from violence and war into the nonviolence and peace of Christ, from fear, hatred, and indifference into the unconditional love and boundless compassion of Christ?

3. Can you spend more time alone with Jesus in prayer, just as he spent time alone in prayer with his beloved God? Can you try to dwell more and more in his light?

4. How are you like the male disciples, sleeping through the transfiguration of Christ? What wakes you up? In what areas of the life, faith, hope, and love do you need to wake up?

5. What does it mean for you to understand your human identity as a beloved son or daughter of the God of love? What keeps you from living your life as a beloved son or daughter of the God of love? How can you deepen your identity as a beloved son or daughter of the God of love?

6. Who are the saints, prophets, and holy ones in your life who encourage you to follow Jesus on the path of love, peace, and compassion?

7. How do you listen to Jesus? What keeps you from listening to Jesus? What does Jesus say to you when you take the time to listen to him? What does Jesus tell his disciples to do when they listen to him? How do you obey his commandments to love one another, forgive one another, love your enemies, and be as compassionate as God?

8. What are you afraid of? How do you respond to Jesus' commandment "Do not be afraid"? How can you move from fear to fearless peace? What keeps you from trusting in Jesus, and how can you trust more and more in him?

9. What would it mean for you to feel the loving touch of Jesus and hear his commandment to "rise!"? What does resurrection mean for you? How can you begin to live as if you are headed toward resurrection? What would it mean for you to practice resurrection in your daily life?

Dear Jesus,

Please wake me up so that I may recognize your transfigured presence.

Help me to live and walk in your light and love.

Help me not to block your journey to the cross but to support and encourage your work for the healing and transformation of the world.

Help me to listen to what you want to say, to obey your commandments of love and compassion, and to take you at your word.

Give me the grace not to be afraid, but to rise up to new life and follow you more closely every day for the rest of my life. Amen.

PART FOUR

DOWN THE MOUNTAIN TO THE CROSS

Steps Along the Transfiguration Journey

1. Notice the ways you have rejected the transfigured Christ and supported the anti-transfiguration culture of violence, injustice, and war.

2. Allow Christ to disarm your heart; commit yourself to Gospel nonviolence; and live today in the light of his peace, love, and compassion.

3. Walk with Jesus down the mountain on the way of the cross. Accompany him on the journey of nonviolent, suffering love in resistance to systemic injustice.

4. Stand up publicly and confront injustice, greed, war, nuclear weapons, and the culture of violence as Jesus did with

steadfast, creative, active nonviolence, and accept the consequences with love and forgiveness.

5. As you walk the way of the cross with Jesus, recall those transfiguration moments in your life and remind yourself of the new life of resurrection and peace to come.

6. Heal those around you. Pray and fast for those in need. Touch the marginalized and oppressed with your compassionate love. Expel the demons of violence and death, and help others live in the Holy Spirit of love and peace.

7. Notice how you resist accompanying Jesus toward the paschal mystery. Pray for the grace to walk all the way with Jesus to the cross through nonviolent resistance to evil, and into the new life of resurrection.

15

Dorothy Day, Pedro Arrupe, and the Anti-Transfiguration

August 6 marks the feast of the Transfiguration. August 6 is also an anti-feast, the anniversary of the demonic U.S. atomic bombing of Hiroshima. At 8:10 A.M. on August 6, 1945, the United States dropped one bomb that vaporized over 140,000 human beings in a flash of bright, white light. Thousands more died in the following weeks from the overshadowing cloud of radiation poisoning. Tens of thousands more died from cancer in the decades that followed.

Three days after Hiroshima, the United States did it again, in Nagasaki, where we vaporized another 50,000 people.

"We dropped the bomb to save lives," the U.S. military announced. Because it knew the Japanese were about to surrender, the United States wanted to show the Soviet Union that it was now number one. This was the ending of World War II and the beginning of the Cold War. Sixty years later, after the collapse of Communism and the Soviet Union, we still keep the world on edge with 30,000 nuclear weapons. We are willing to kill as many people as necessary to maintain our global economic, political, and military domination.

When read in the context of the nuclear blast over Hiroshima, the story of Jesus' transfiguration takes on added meaning. The Gospel not only shows us the flip side of our nuclear violence in the nonviolence of Jesus but offers us a way out of our insanity. It contrasts Jesus and the God of nonviolence with our violent selves and our desire to dominate others. The Transfiguration portrays the inner power of Jesus' transforming nonviolence—pure love, perfect peace, unconditional mercy, and steadfast resistance to the forces of violence. In his transfiguration, Jesus radiates perfect nonviolence. In the Transfiguration, we glimpse the glorious face of the God of peace and begin to understand who Jesus is and what it means to follow him. Through his inner prayer, Jesus undergoes a spiritual explosion of love and peace that leads him to resist the structures of injustice—even to the point of death—and reveal the God of nonviolence.

The U.S. atomic bombings of Hiroshima and Nagasaki, by contrast, reveal the exact opposite of God's transfiguring nonviolence. They epitomize our disfiguring violence. Two Christians who understood the demonic horror of U.S. nuclear weapons were Dorothy Day and Pedro Arrupe. They understood both the Transfiguration and Hiroshima, and spoke out prophetically against war and nuclear weapons. Their lives outline the discipleship journey. They show us how to be Christian in the nuclear age. They urge us to work for the abolition of nuclear weapons and war itself for the sake of nonviolent, transfigured Jesus.

Dorothy Day, an Instrument of Christ's Peace

Reading the Gospel from the perspective of the bomb, with its bright flash of white light, its mushroom cloud, and its nuclear fireball incinerating our sisters and brothers, Dorothy Day called the bombing of Hiroshima an "anti-transfiguration." In Jesus, she saw the possibility of humanity's transfiguration through the way of contemplative nonviolence. With Hiroshima, however, she saw our preference for disfiguring violence.

Dorothy Day spent her days quietly listening to the words of Jesus and then living out his message of service to the poor and promoting justice and peace. This prayerful attention to Jesus transfigured her life. Day's contemplative nonviolence made her an instrument of Christ's peace. Without her prayerful listening, the Catholic Worker movement would not have begun or flourished. Today the Catholic Worker has over 140 houses of hospitality for the homeless and inspires thousands of Christians to work full-time for justice and peace.

In the days after the bombing of Hiroshima and Nagasaki, Dorothy Day wrote a scathing denunciation of President Truman's celebration of the bombings and our willingness to incinerate people.

Mr. Truman was jubilant. He went from table to table on the cruiser which was bringing him home from the Big Three conference, telling the great news. "Jubilant" the newspapers said. Jubilate Deo. We have killed hundreds of thousands of Japanese. That is, we hope we have killed them, the Associated Press, on page one, column one, of the *Herald Tribune* says. The effect is hoped for,

not known. It is to be hoped that they are vaporized, our
Japanese sisters and brothers, scattered, men, women
and babies, to the four winds, over the seven seas.
Perhaps we will breathe their dust into our nostrils, feel
them in the fog of New York in our faces, feel them in
the rains on the hills of New Jersey. President Truman
was jubilant. We have created destruction.

Our Lord himself has already pronounced judgment
on the atomic bomb. When James and John wished to
call down fire from heaven on their enemies, Jesus
turned and rebuked them. "You know not of what spirit
you are. The Son of Humanity came not to destroy souls
but to save. Inasmuch as you have done it to one of the
least of these sisters and brothers of mine, you have
done it to me." (*The Catholic Worker*, September 1945)

After the Japanese attack on Pearl Harbor, Day wrote an
open plea for Christians to stand up and resist U.S. warmaking.
She saw as few have that war would bring not peace but only
death and more war.

All wars are, by their very nature, evil and destructive. It
has become too late for civilized people to accept this
evil. We must take a stand. We must renounce war as an
instrument of policy. We must affirm that there will be
no more war. Never, ever again. War is hunger, thirst,
blindness and death. I call you to resist it. You young
men should refuse to take up arms. You young women
should tear down the patriotic posters. And all of you,
young and old, should put away your flags. (from a talk
given in New York City, December 8, 1941)

While she condemned nuclear violence as the anti-transfiguration, Day also wrote about the power of nonviolent love, which explodes in the transfiguration of Jesus. In the conclusion of her biography of St. Thérèse of Lisieux, advocate of the little way of suffering love, Day argued that the power of love, even in the smallest act, is more powerful than any nuclear weapon.

> Therese of Lisieux practiced the presence of God and she did all things—all the little things that make up our daily life and contact with others—for God's honor and glory. She did not need much time to expound what she herself called "her little way," which she said was for all. She wrote her story, and God did the rest.... What stands out in her life? Her holiness of course. With governments becoming stronger and more centralized, ordinary people feel ineffective. When the whole world seems given over to preparedness for war and the show of force, the message of Therese is quite a different one. She speaks to our condition. Is the atom a small thing? And yet what havoc it has wrought. Is her little way a small contribution to the life of the spirit? It has all the power of the spirit of Christianity behind it. It is an explosive force that can transform our lives and the life of the world, once put into effect. (Day, *Therese*, [Notre Dame, Ind.: Fides, 1960], 174–75)

Pedro Arrupe, A Witness of Christ's Truth

On the outskirts of Hiroshima at the time of the bombing, there stood a small Jesuit novitiate where young Japanese novices were trained in prayer and service to the poor. At that time, the novice master was a charismatic doctor from the Basque country of Spain, Father Pedro Arrupe, who would, in 1965, become the most important Superior General of the Society of Jesus since St. Ignatius himself. On August 6, immediately after the bombing, Arrupe and his novices began caring for survivors. They turned the novitiate into a makeshift hospital, where hundreds of sick people recovered from radiation sickness. Because of Arrupe's attention, most of them survived.

In the next few years, before he became provincial of the Japanese Jesuits in 1959, Pedro Arrupe traveled the world three times, giving over one thousand lectures about those dark days in Hiroshima and the urgent spiritual reasons for total nuclear disarmament. Eventually, he wrote about his experience on the morning of August 6, 1945:

The roof tiles, bits of glass and beams had scarcely ceased falling, and the deafening roar died away, when I rose from the ground and saw before me the wall clock still hanging in its place but motionless. Its pendulum seemed nailed down. It was ten minutes past eight. For me that silent and motionless clock has been a symbol. The explosion of the first atomic bomb has become a para-historical phenomenon. The pendulum stopped and Hiroshima has remained engraved on my mind. It has no relation with time. It belongs to motionless eternity.

The oven of Hiroshima has become a fixed satellite in the stratosphere, accompanying the earth in its course around the sun. It is a latter-day Sword of Damocles hanging over humanity. Its sinister light, capable of destroying the retina of anyone staring it in the face, is an illuminating and discriminating power greater than that of the X-ray. In the midst of so much destruction, confusion and corruption, the dark mystery of atomic radiation renders the screen of humanity clarescent, revealing both the fleshly futility of that which disappears like a shadow, and the solidity, firmer than bone, of spiritual values.

Who can guarantee that no nation will unleash an atomic explosion to obtain its political or national ends? Given our experience of our humanity, there can never be a guarantee that atomic bombs will not be used so long as they exist in the arsenals of some countries. The only trustworthy guarantee of their non-use will be their non-existence. (Arrupe, *A Planet to Heal* [Rome: Ignatian Center for Spirituality, 1975])

Today, the ruins of Hiroshima offer us a choice: the choice between transfiguration and anti-transfiguration, nonviolence and nonexistence, life and death. In the light of the transfigured Jesus, the God of peace, and the Gospel call to nonviolence, North American Christians name the crucifixion of Hiroshima and Nagasaki by our government not just sinful, unjust, and immoral, but demonic—an evil act by a people (ourselves) possessed by the spirits of violence. We apologize to the people of Hiroshima and Nagasaki for vaporizing them and unleashing the nuclear age, and in a spirit of repentance, we pledge ourselves anew to the pursuit of nuclear disarmament, the abolition of war, and a world without weapons or hunger. We promise, from now on, to listen to the gentle voice of the God of nonviolence.

At the end of his talks, Pedro Arrupe said:

History shows that neither war nor violent revolution have ever solved humanity's problems, nor will they ever. They are born of hatred, and though hatred harms, it does not heal. It can never be a human solution. The new atomic weapons, exponentially increasing humanity's destruction potential for fratricidal conflict, have made us realize how terrible hatred is and have aroused our horror of it. But it is as terrible when it employs the bow, the sling or the sword as when it makes use of multi-megaton atomic bombs. What is deadly and truly terrible about force and violence is not so much their destructive effects as the hatred which spawns them. Hatred, faintly discernible in the struggles of primitive humanity, is the same hatred which horrifies us when it is amplified millions of times over in atomic explosions. Neither gunpowder nor dynamite nor atomic power would destroy humanity if there were not hatred. A disease is terrifying so long as it cannot be cured for lack of a proper diagnosis or remedy. A diagnosis of war and violence shows that they are the effects of the virus of hatred. The antidote for hatred is what we call love, and the effect of love is the counter-sign of war: peace.

When will humanity discover that in the core of people there lives the divine reality? For this humanity will need a flash of light far more powerful than that which blinded us at Hiroshima: the light of faith which illumines without blinding because it is both powerful and gentle. On that day, when humanity discovers through the light of faith in God and in all people, and sees that this God does indeed live and is a God of love, wars and violence will cease and hatred will be no more.

God will be seen as the cause of true union and human happiness. On that day will be born a new humanity, the children of God. (Arrupe, *A Planet to Heal*)

Peace, Not an Optional Commitment

On August 6, 2002, at the annual remembrance ceremonies in Hiroshima, Mayor Tadatoshi Akiba criticized the United States "for unilaterally pursuing its own interests" and urged "a worldwide ban on weapons of mass destruction. The United States has no right to force Pax Americana on the rest of us, or to unilaterally determine the fate of the world," he said from Ground Zero nearly a year after the September 11 attacks. "The probability that nuclear weapons will be used again and the danger of nuclear war are increasing. Since the terrorist attack against the American people on September 11 last year, the danger has become more striking."

"As the only country in history to have experienced atomic bombings," Japan's prime minister, Junichiro Koizumi, said, "I would like to underline Japan's unwavering commitment to its war-renouncing constitution and its three principles: no possession, non-production, and non-entry of nuclear weapons."

In 1984, the U.S. Catholic bishops concluded their pastoral letter on peace with a call for nuclear disarmament. "The whole world must summon the moral courage and technical means to say 'no' to weapons of mass destruction; 'no' to an arms trade which robs the poor and the vulnerable; and 'no' to the moral danger of a nuclear age which places before humankind indefensible choices of constant terror or surrender. Peacemaking is not an optional commitment. It is a requirement of our faith. We are called to be peacemakers, not by some movement of the moment, but by our Lord Jesus" ("The Challenge of Peace," no. 333).

The story of the Transfiguration is not a pious myth reserved for a few religious fanatics or Scripture scholars. Set against the frightening reality of today's wars, nuclear weapons, and global violence, it is a last-ditch call from the God of peace to adopt Jesus' spirituality of nonviolence and to reject our potential for total nuclear destruction once and for all.

My friend Philip Berrigan spent over four years in prison for his opposition to the Vietnam War. On the feast of the Transfiguration, August 6, 1968, he wrote from prison on the choice before us, the choice of transfiguring nonviolence or disfiguring nuclear violence:

A study in contrast—the transfiguration of divine mercy on the Mount, and the anti-transfiguration of human arrogance and pitilessness at Hiroshima. God struck his tent in Christ's human flesh, whose shining face spoke of divine power and compassion, while the fireball at Hiroshima consumed everyone it could reach and blinded onlookers many miles away. It came, carefully stamped, "Made in the USA," a curious response by allegedly Christian people to God's imperative, "Listen to him!" Can a nation recover from a mental lapse like Hiroshima, or more fundamentally, from a disintegration of humanity that made Hiroshima a fateful climax of moral bankruptcy? One can only hope that it can. Our course of transfigurations has not changed, almost as if what we are really at war with is the divine mercy itself. (Philip Berrigan, *Prison Journals of a Priest Revolutionary* [New York: Holt, Rinehart and Winston, 1970], 77)

To follow Jesus on the path of transfiguring nonviolence, we have to leave our lofty heights, comfortable safety, and private spiritualities and go with him down the mountain into the world of war, where we must confront the structures of violence head-on. The real discipleship journey begins now, after the Transfiguration, as we follow Jesus on the road to Jerusalem.

16

Down the Mountain with Jesus

A fter the disciples hear the command to rise and not be afraid, they stand up and follow Jesus down the mountain. They had seen his glorious transformation and heard the voice of God, and now they have no choice but to follow Jesus, even though they do not know what just happened.

Going down the mountain, the disciples are still confused and afraid. They do not understand what they have seen and heard. They do not know why Jesus is going to Jerusalem. They fear what this might mean for themselves. But they know they have to follow him. The voice of God told them bluntly to listen attentively to Jesus from now on.

This is the third movement of the Transfiguration. After we climb up the mountain with Jesus and witness the Transfiguration on the mountaintop, we follow him down the mountain into the world to confront injustice and proclaim

God's reign. The disciples have to turn and face the world. They have to enter the struggle for justice and peace, challenge the world's injustice and violence, and put their faith into action precisely because Jesus does.

The same is true for us. After we encounter the transfigured Jesus, hear the voice of God, and listen to the teachings of Jesus, we too must turn and face the world. We would prefer not to. We do not want to get involved in the messy business of corruption, greed, ego, division, racism, sexism, violence, war, poverty, and injustice. We want to mind our own business, earn our pay, and tend to our families. But as followers of Jesus, we have to go down the mountain and face the world, just as he did.

Don't Tell Anyone About the Vision

After the voice speaks from the cloud, the disciples look around and see no one with them but Jesus. He appears the same as he did before. "As they were coming down from the mountain," Matthew writes, "Jesus charged them, 'Do not tell the vision to anyone until the Son of Humanity has been raised from the dead' " (17:9). Only Matthew uses the word "vision" to describe the Transfiguration. "As they were coming down from the mountain," Mark records, "he charged them not to relate what they had seen to anyone, except when the Son of Humanity had risen from the dead. So they kept the matter to themselves, questioning what rising from the dead meant" (9:9–10).

The disciples do not understand transfiguration or resurrection. They cannot comprehend that Jesus will be executed and rise from the dead. They still do not know who he is. They probably do not understand his title Son of Humanity or the name given him from the cloud, "my beloved Son." Few people had any notion of resurrection in those days. These fishermen certainly cannot grasp these images. Only later, when they experience his resurrection firsthand, will they be able to proclaim this mystery.

Jesus does not want Peter, James, or John to tell anyone what they saw until his resurrection because he knows that they do not understand the Transfiguration, that they will not be able to explain it, and that people will not be able to accept it. It will seem utterly unbelievable, and probably prevent people from growing in faith. Only after his resurrection, when they themselves see that he has overcome death, will the story of the Transfiguration and their testimony be convincing. Perhaps the disciples are relieved not to have to discuss what happened on the mountain.

The Question About Elijah

But the disciples are still confused. They cannot grasp Jesus' talk about resurrection. They still cannot fathom the vision of Elijah and Moses they witnessed, or the voice they heard from the cloud. So they start to ask questions. They ask themselves what resurrection means; then they ask Jesus about Elijah's second coming. "Then the disciples asked him, 'Why do the scribes say that Elijah must come first?'" Matthew writes. "He said in reply, 'Elijah will indeed come and restore all things; but I tell you that Elijah has already come, and they did not recognize him but did to him whatever they pleased. So also will the Son of Humanity suffer at their hands.' Then the disciples un-

derstood that he was speaking to them of John the Baptist"
(17:10–13).

Mark's version features nearly the same account, except that
Jesus changes the subject even more abruptly, from the question
about Elijah to his own question about his upcoming crucifixion. "Elijah will indeed come first and restore all things," Jesus
tells them, "yet how is it written regarding the Son of Humanity
that he must suffer greatly and be treated with contempt? But I
tell you that Elijah has come and they did to him whatever they
pleased, as it is written of him" (9:12–13).

The disciples ask about Elijah because they learned from
the scribes that, according to the last verse in the Hebrew
Scriptures, in the Book of Malachi, God promised to send the
prophet Elijah to prepare the Messiah's coming. "Lo, I will send
you Elijah, the prophet, before the day of the Lord comes, the
great and terrible day" (3:24). Jesus confirms the Scripture and
announces that Elijah did indeed come in the person of John
the Baptist, but then he turns their question toward his own inevitable suffering and death. Just as the authorities arrested and
killed Elijah in John the Baptist, they will arrest and kill him.
Jesus remains focused on the cross, but the disciples are confused, so he tries to prepare them for his arrest, torture, and crucifixion. How is it that the Son of Humanity must suffer? he asks
them. Because this is the only question that matters, he turns
them to the Scriptures for clues about his suffering and death.
Later, Luke will recount how the risen Jesus "opened the scriptures" to the disciples and explained everything that was written about him (Luke 24:27; 24:45).

Like the disciples, we may be afraid and confused. We may
listen to modern-day scribes who teach literal interpretations of

the Scriptures for simplistic, clear-cut answers. But Jesus points us instead to the struggle for justice and its outcome on the cross. We can discuss mystical experience and fundamentalist interpretations, but Jesus would prefer that we walk with him down the mountain and take up the journey to Jerusalem and the cross. He wants us to be willing to suffer without retaliating in the struggle for justice and peace, to lay down our lives for suffering humanity, and to follow him on the path to martyrdom for the coming of God's reign of peace. Then we will understand the meaning of the cross, the resurrection, and the Transfiguration.

Perhaps the best step we can take is to heed the voice from the cloud, humbly listen to Jesus, follow him on the journey, and let him teach us the wisdom of the cross.

The Road to Jerusalem

Jesus proceeds down the mountain with one goal in mind: to challenge corruption in the Jerusalem Temple. He talks about the cross and the resurrection. As his disciples, we need to walk down the mountain in his footsteps and head toward our own modern-day Jerusalems. We must see the cross and resurrection that loom ahead of us. We have to enter Jesus' paschal mystery if we want to see his transfiguring glory.

This will not be easy. To follow Jesus faithfully, we have to recognize the systemic, institutionalized injustice around us and then confront it, resist it, and convert it through transfiguring nonviolence. This journey requires prayer, listening, discernment, study, community, discipline, and commitment.

Over the past twenty-five years, I have tried to identify my

Jerusalem and risk there the cross of nonviolent resistance to injustice. Growing up around Washington, D.C., the capital of the most violent nation in the world, made my search easy. On countless occasions, I faced the White House, the U.S. Capitol, the Pentagon, the Department of Energy, the Department of Justice, and the State Department at prayer vigils and demonstrations, and was arrested at each of them for acts of nonviolent civil disobedience on behalf of justice and peace. Around the country, I have journeyed to Lawrence Livermore National Laboratory; the Strategic Air Command Base in Omaha; West Point; Bath Iron Works in Maine; the Presidio Army Base in San Francisco; the Trident submarine bases in Florida, Connecticut, and Washington; the School of the Americas; the U.S. Mission to the United Nations; Riverside Research Institute for Star Wars in Manhattan; the USS *Intrepid*; the Concord Naval Weapons Station; various death-row prisons; and federal buildings in Los Angeles and San Francisco. In each case, my friends and I tried to turn over the tables of injustice and call for conversion to the God of peace. Unfortunately, our witness has not been accepted. But we refuse to give up.

Over the last few years, living and working among low-income parishes in New Mexico, I have organized a campaign to disarm Los Alamos National Laboratory, the birthplace of the atomic bomb. As a follower of Jesus, I realize I cannot remain safely in my own Galilee without facing the injustice around me. And there is no greater injustice than Los Alamos, where thousands of good people plan the greatest evil–the vaporization of millions of people and the destruction of the planet. Los Alamos consumes millions of dollars every year for the research, development, and maintenance of weapons of mass destruction. My discipleship journey–going down the mountain with Jesus–leads me to confront this injustice with steadfast nonviolence, regardless of the personal consequences.

Training in Discipleship Nonviolence

For over three years, Jesus trained his disciples in the practice of active nonviolence. Every day with Jesus was a spiritual retreat about the way of nonviolence. His catechism of nonviolence taught them the wisdom of nonviolence as well as prepared them for their own inevitable confrontations with the authorities and possible arrest and martyrdom. "I am sending you like sheep into a world of wolves," he told them (Matthew 10:16).

As we go down the mountain with Jesus to face a world of injustice, we too need to be ready. Although we stand on the shoulders of the apostles, the saints, the martyrs, and our own modern-day prophets, we are surrounded by a culture of war, where violence runs deep. Because we are intimidated into believing in violence, supporting violence, and practicing violence, we easily become addicted to violence and do not even know it. Over and over again, we have to relearn the lessons of Gospel nonviolence if we dare face a world of wolves as Jesus, the Lamb of God, did so well. We have to turn to the Higher Power, renounce our violence, accept the sobriety of nonviolence, take to the streets with God's way of creative love, just as the first apostles eventually did, and try to disarm the world.

"On the peak of Tabor next to Christ transfigured," Archbishop Oscar Romero preached shortly before his assassination, "the five men who appear–Moses, Elijah, Peter, James and John–are men of violent character, and they committed terribly violent acts. Moses killed an Egyptian. Elijah put to the sword the prophets who did not adore the true God. Peter drew his word against Malchus. James and John begged Christ to rain fire on a town that would not give him lodging. But I say, Christians are peacemakers, not because they cannot fight, but because they prefer the force of peace." Archbishop Romero taught his suffering people the wisdom of nonviolence.

The art of nonviolence requires training, just as the art of war requires training. For years, the peace movement has been training people in the tactics, strategies, and theories of active nonviolence. My experience teaching nonviolence around the country shows me that we are all in constant need of further study, training, and practice in Gospel nonviolence. Any public nonviolent action, like Jesus' long march to Jerusalem, requires discernment, prayer, community, organization, and preparation. Every great witness of nonviolence in the last century came after long preparation. It usually did not spring up overnight. From the People Power movement in the Philippines to the antiapartheid work of the churches in South Africa, people prepared themselves to challenge injustice in a spirit of steadfast nonviolence, like Jesus.

When my friends and I walked onto the Seymour Johnson Air Force Base near Goldsboro, North Carolina, on December 7, 1993, to disrupt war games and hammer on an unarmed nuclear-capable F-15 fighter bomber, we did it after years of preparation. For over a decade, I studied, prayed over, and planned for this act of nonviolent disarmament. I knew that my actions could lead to twenty years of imprisonment, so I had to be prepared. My friends and I spent a dozen weekends together studying, discussing, and practicing nonviolence before that fateful morning. We prayed, read the Scriptures, shared our fears, and analyzed the weapons. We engaged in role playing so that we could respond to the armed soldiers with instinctive nonviolence. We were going down the mountain to a terrible Jerusalem, and we wanted to be as ready as possible.

Before embarking on the famous salt march to the sea on March 12, 1930, in a campaign for independence, Mahatma Gandhi and seventy other companions spent over two years in full-time preparation. They fasted and prayed together. They read the Scriptures, experimented with personal nonviolence, and prepared themselves for arrest and even death. They engaged in role playing so that they would respond naturally without violence, but with truth and love, to the British soldiers and police.

When the day came for their 240-mile walk to the beach at Dandi, where Gandhi intended to pick up a handful of salt in violation of British law, they had no idea what would happen. They expected to be arrested immediately, if not shot on sight. They also suspected their march would be ignored by everyone, including the media and the international movement, but they were determined to walk the road to freedom and take the risk no matter what. Like Jesus, they went down the mountain and walked the road to the sea, where they engaged in dramatic civil disobedience.

Within days, the country caught fire with excitement. When Gandhi arrived at the shore and called upon the nation to break the British laws in a campaign for a "free India," over 300 million Indians joined him. Thousands, including Gandhi, were arrested. A few days later, Gandhi's *satyagrahis*, trained in "truth-force," marched upon the Dharasana Salt Works. This time, the British clubbed them with steel rods, injuring hundreds, killing several of them. But not one of Gandhi's associates backed off or retaliated with violence.

Their training paid off. They were faithful to the way of non-violence. The whole of India, as well as Britain and the world, was shocked at the brutality of the British and the willing, innocent suffering of the unarmed satyagrahis. Because they refused to fight back, their pain and suffering caused a global outcry and sealed the end of the Raj. Within a few years, more than 300,000 Indians were imprisoned for acts of nonviolent civil disobedience. When the British finally left, they did so as "friends," as Gandhi had hoped. That momentary national transfiguration was possible only because of the steadfast nonviolence practiced by the Indian resisters.

Martin Luther King, Jr., learned from Gandhi the importance of nonviolence training before direct action. During his campaigns to break the segregation laws, he and his colleagues held countless training sessions before tens of thousands throughout the South. In Montgomery, Greensboro, Nashville, Albany, Atlanta, Jackson, Birmingham, and Selma, activists taught one another how to endure yelling, spitting, beatings, dog bites, fire hoses, arrest, jail, and death threats without resorting to further violence but still insisting on the truth of racial equality. Their willingness to suffer for the cause of justice forced the country to dismantle segregation and enact civil rights legislation.

The turning point came during the Birmingham campaign in the spring of 1963. Dr. King, as did many other activists, spent a memorable Holy Week in jail. But the campaign was weakening. The media were not paying attention to their park protest. King decided to allow children and high school students to take to the streets for racial justice. The young people were eager to join the campaign. Before they walked toward Sheriff Bull Connor's German shepherds and fire hoses, each person signed a "Commitment Card," pledging to remain faithful to the way of nonviolence no matter what happened. Indeed, hundreds were attacked and hurt, but none responded with violence. Within days, firemen and police officers refused to attack the marchers any further.

The pledge made a world of difference. It was written by Rev. James Lawson, my co-worker at the Fellowship of Reconciliation. Dr. King called Jim the greatest teacher of nonviolence in the world. Jim still maintains that everyone everywhere needs to make a similar commitment to active nonviolence:

> I hereby pledge myself–my person and body–to the nonviolent movement. Therefore, I will keep the following ten commandments:
>
> 1. Meditate daily on the teachings and life of Jesus.
> 2. Remember always that the nonviolent seeks justice and reconciliation, not victory.
> 3. Walk and talk in the manner of love, for God is love.
> 4. Pray daily to be used by God in order that all people might be free.
> 5. Sacrifice personal wishes in order that all people might be free.
> 6. Observe with both friend and foe the ordinary rules of courtesy.
> 7. Seek to perform regular service for others and for the world.
> 8. Refrain from the violence of fist, tongue, or heart.
> 9. Strive to be in good spiritual and bodily health.
> 10. Follow the directions of the movement and the captain on a demonstration. (King, *Why We Can't*

Wait [New York: New American Library, 1964], 63–64)

Going down the mountain with Jesus is like marching toward the Dharasana Salt Works or confronting the Birmingham police dogs. Jesus turned and took the road to Jerusalem in a similar costly campaign of nonviolent resistance to imperial and religious injustice. He knew such public direct action on the outskirts of the brutal empire could only result in arrest, imprisonment, trial, torture, and execution. He had prepared himself and his disciples for this daring nonviolence. He knew that God would remain faithful to him, and that God wanted him to embark on this new exodus, as Moses called it. He set out, and the disciples followed him as far as they could. As his disciples, we too must follow him on the way of the cross and practice the power of transfiguring nonviolence.

At some point in our lives, we too have to start down the mountain and take the road to Jerusalem. We have to move from mystical spiritual experience to public, political action for justice and peace on behalf of the poor and oppressed. We know the outcome. We may be dismissed, harassed, and ignored. Our efforts may appear to end in failure. Our lives may be disrupted. Worse, we might be arrested, imprisoned, even killed. But if we follow Jesus, we will one day realize the promise of resurrection and see his glorious, transfigured face.

And so, we take another step on the discipleship journey down the mountain to the cross.

17.

_____

The Healing Touch of Transfiguration

Traditionally, the story of the Transfiguration on the mountaintop has been connected with what happened at the bottom of the mountain. According to each synoptic Gospel, there Jesus dramatically healed a boy possessed by a demon. But after the glowing experience on the mountaintop, Jesus was disappointed to discover the rest of the disciples arguing among themselves, unable to heal, and failing to follow him. After his initial exasperation, he called them once again to pray and believe.

"When they came to the disciples, they saw a large crowd around them and scribes arguing with them," Mark writes. "Immediately on seeing him, the whole crowd was utterly amazed. They ran up to him and greeted him. He asked them, 'What are you arguing about with them?' Someone from the crowd answered him, 'Teacher, I have brought to you my son possessed by a mute spirit. Wherever it seizes him, it throws

him down; he foams at the mouth, grinds his teeth, and becomes rigid. I asked your disciples to drive it out, but they were
unable to do so' " (9:14–18).

On the mountaintop, the disciples slept through his transfiguration, babbled on to gain control of the situation, trembled in
fear and terror, and questioned themselves and Jesus. Now, at
the foot of the mountain, they argue among themselves and
with the authorities while flunking the test of healing a possessed boy. These pathetic images of incompetent discipleship
by and large sum up the Church today. We too sleep through
the Transfiguration, try to control God, tremble in fear, question ourselves and God, argue among ourselves and with religious leaders–and all the while fail to expel the demons of
death and heal the poor. Most priests, ministers, bishops, cardinals, and other religious leaders have become CEOs who prefer dealing with lawyers, bankers, and fund-raisers to maintain
their power, prestige, privilege, and control. Few church people
today try to expel the demons of violence, poverty, racism, sexism, war, and nuclear weapons. Few serve the world's suffering
children. Few dare risk the cross by denouncing systemic injustice and breaking unjust laws that violate God's law. Few rock
the boat.

"They brought the boy to him," Mark continues. "And when
he saw him, the spirit immediately threw the boy into convulsions. As he fell to the ground, he began to roll around and
foam at the mouth. Then he questioned his father, 'How long
has this been happening to him?' He replied, 'Since childhood.
It has often thrown him into fire and into water to kill him. But
if you can do anything, have compassion on us and help us.'
Jesus said to him, 'If you can! Everything is possible to one who
has faith.' Then the boy's father cried out, 'I do believe, help my

unbelief!' Jesus, on seeing a crowd rapidly gathering, rebuked the unclean spirit and said to it, 'Mute and deaf spirit, I command you: come out of him and never enter him again!' Shouting and throwing the boy into convulsions, it came out. He became like a corpse, which caused many to say, 'He is dead!' But Jesus took him by the hand, raised him, and he stood up" (9:20–27).

This astounding story is loaded with symbolic details. First, the deadly demon leaves the boy on the ground rigid, as if dead. Mark is telling us about the power of death, the imperial forces of violence, which kill the poor around the world. The greatest, most deadly force, then and now, is war. It possesses us, takes us over, leads us to scream and shout, induces us to murder and support mass murder, leaves us rigid, and kills our spirit. Next, Jesus acts like the perfect psychologist. He asks the father how long the boy has been possessed. He learns that the possession began in childhood. Then Mark uses the symbols of the early Church to explain how "the demon" is actually attacking not just the boy but the Church itself. The demons of the imperial culture of violence always try to co-opt Christ's symbols of life to bring death. In this case, the demons try to burn the boy in an anti-Pentecost. Then they try to drown him in an anti-baptism. Instead of bringing life, the Christian symbols of fire and water, representing new life and the Holy Spirit, are misused to bring death. The lesson is that anything that leads to violence and death is not of God; it is demonic.

Next, the father issues a touching plea that the disciples themselves never utter. The father intervenes, begs for compassion, and asks for help. "I believe, help my unbelief," he pleads, summing up the disposition of a true disciple—affirming faith in Jesus while begging for mercy in light of our need for greater faith. Finally, Jesus speaks with authority over the demons of death. He commands the evil spirit to leave. People initially think the boy is dead, but Jesus takes him by the hand and raises him up. We too rise when Jesus expels the demons of death. We experience resurrection and become people of resurrection. In the end, whether we are unfaithful disciples or possessed people, Jesus will call us to rise.

"When he entered the house, his disciples asked him in private, 'Why could we not drive it out?' He said to them, 'This kind can only come out through prayer.' They left from there and began a journey . . ." (Mark 9:28–30).

Matthew's version offers a slightly different twist on the disciples' inability to drive out the demons of death. "Because of your little faith," Jesus answers them. "Amen, I say to you, if you have faith the size of a mustard seed, you will say to this mountain, 'Move from here to there,' and it will move. Nothing will be impossible for you" (17:20).

Prayer and Faith

Earlier, Jesus had missioned these disciples to expel the demons of death just as he had done (Mark 1:32, 6:12). Initially, Mark says, they were able to do this, but now they have failed. The Evangelists explain that they are unable to expel the demons of violence because they lack contemplative prayer and deep faith. "This kind can only come out through prayer," Mark's Jesus says. "Because of your little faith," Matthew's Jesus asserts. These are powerful indictments as well as invitations to the disciples—and us—to follow Jesus in his work of expelling demons by becoming people of prayer and faith, people filled with his Holy Spirit.

Prayer and faith are critically important for the work of dis-arming, transfiguring nonviolence. Unlike Jesus, the disciples are full of doubt and violence. They try to win the approval of the establishment. They argue with the scribes in an effort to prove themselves, but in the process, they fail in their mission to expel the demons of death and heal those in need. Instead of revealing themselves as faithful people of contemplative nonvi-olence, they demonstrate that, like the scribes, they are filled with violence. Their inner violence prevents them from healing others and doing the work of Jesus.

Jesus, by contrast, does not have a trace of violence inside him. He is perfectly nonviolent, the embodiment of healing love and divine peace. In this world of violence, his nonviolent presence is healing. People are disarmed and healed just by touching him. With his radiant, glowing nonviolence, Jesus commands the demons of violence to flee. He can expel the demons of violence because he is full of transfiguring nonvio-lence. He holds perfect faith in his beloved God and practices daily contemplative prayer. He does not cultivate the evil spir-its of the Roman Empire, the military, the governing rulers, the rebellious Zealots, or the religious authorities. He is filled with the Holy Spirit. Because he is so filled with God, his body ex-plodes with light and grace on the mountaintop. Now, at the bottom of the mountain, he heals those who are being crushed by imperial violence. Likewise, he wants us to be filled with God's Holy Spirit so that we can radiate healing love and peace. He wants us to join him in that campaign of nonviolent action, to expel the culture's demonic violence and shine with glowing, transfiguring nonviolence.

To do this, the Gospels insist, we must deepen our prayer and our faith. We cannot heal those possessed by the culture's violence, wars, and nuclear demons until we ourselves are freed from violence. We cannot help others trapped by the culture if we carry within us the sludge of the culture. The only way to rid ourselves of inner violence and the culture's control is with the spiritual tools of prayer and faith. Some ancient Marcan texts also include fasting. The Gospels call us to turn to God in prayer and fasting, focus on God, and be filled with the Holy Spirit. Then the evil spirits of the culture that drive us to hurt one another, hurt ourselves, and wage war will be driven away from us. We will be disarmed and healed. And once we are healed, we can become, like Jesus, instruments of his disarming, healing nonviolence.

The Gospels challenge us to be people of great faith, to know that nothing is impossible with God, and to move mountains. The Evangelists urge us to act with the same bold faith as Jesus, to address the mountains of injustice, and to move them aside so that God's reign of peace stands in our midst for all to see.

The Scripture scholar Ched Myers writes about Mark's call to prayer and faith:

> To pray is to learn to believe in a transformation of self and world, which seems, empirically, impossible—as in "moving mountains" (11:23). What is unbelief but the despair, dictated by the dominant powers, that nothing can really change, a despair that renders revolutionary vision and practice impotent. The disciples are instructed to battle this impotence, this temptation to resignation, through prayer. "Keep awake and pray, that you may not succumb to temptation!," Jesus later will urge them (14:38). The "strength" or (inability) to cast out demons

is deeply connected to the "strength to stay awake" (14:37); tragically, the disciples will sleep while Jesus sweats in prayer in Gethsemane, and they will flee when he turns to face the powers. By introducing prayer at this stage of the narrative, is not Mark trying to suggest that he understands it to be the practice of critical reflection upon the "demons within"? Is not prayer the intensely personal struggle within each disciple, and among us collectively, to resist the despair and distractions that cause us to practice unbelief, to abandon or avoid the way of Jesus? And has not this demon, so embedded in our imperial culture, kept us impotent, docile subjects of the status quo "since childhood"? (9:21) (Myers, *Binding the Strong Man* [New York: Orbis Books, 1988], 255–56)

Jesus wants us to liberate one another from the imperial culture of violence that has seeped deep into our souls since childhood. He wants to disarm and heal us, and send us forth to do his work of disarming, healing nonviolence. He wants us to follow him on the road to Jerusalem and disarm the imperial structures of war and injustice, to carry on his gospel campaign by expelling the demons of violence throughout the culture of war.

If we are to expel the demons of death, we have to be filled with Christ's Holy Spirit of life. If we are to disarm the evil spirits of war, we have to radiate the Holy Spirit of Christ's peace. If we are to dismantle the structures of violence, we have to become apostles of contemplative, active, and prophetic nonviolence. Then, we will be able to follow Jesus faithfully on the road to Jerusalem—even to the cross and the new life of resurrection. Because we are temples of the Holy Spirit, our very presence will heal and disarm others, just like Jesus did. Not only will we move mountains but we will end wars, topple empires, beat swords into plowshares, transform enemies into friends, and radiate God's reign of peace.

18.

_____

Heading Toward the Paschal Mystery

G oing down the mountain with Jesus and following him to our own modern-day Jerusalems is not easy. After all, who wants to face injustice, cause a scene, be denounced as unpatriotic, make trouble, and disrupt the culture?

When I was imprisoned in North Carolina for eight months after a Plowshares disarmament action, my friend Joan Chittister wrote me that she found my action difficult to accept, but she understood it and supported it because she knew that, in the end, Christians are called to share the paschal mystery of Jesus. I found her words insightful and helpful. To work for peace and justice, to welcome God's reign of peace on earth, to put the Gospel into practice, we have to enter the paschal mystery of Jesus. We have to risk the cross and resurrection in our own lives. We have to give our lives to nonviolent, suffering love for the whole human race and the creation of a new, nonviolent, more just world. We have to experience the power of redemptive, transforming love and truth, which rises from compassionate, suffering love. We too have to participate in the death and new life of Jesus.

Throughout my life, I have tried to figure out what it means to follow Jesus on the road to Jerusalem and the cross. In 1982, that meant literally journeying to Jerusalem. There I witnessed the reality of war and unexpectedly committed myself to the Gospel of peace and nonviolence. After entering the Jesuits, that meant walking from Georgetown University one April morning to the Pentagon, where I sat down and blocked the main entrance to protest U.S. war-making in my first act of civil disobedience and my first arrest. Later, it meant traveling the world's war zones from El Salvador to Guatemala and Nicaragua to Haiti and Palestine to the Philippines and Northern Ireland. Then it meant walking with Philip Berrigan onto the Seymour Johnson Air Force Base in Goldsboro, North Carolina, to hammer on a nuclear fighter bomber and go to jail. In 1999, while serving as the director of the Fellowship of Reconciliation, it meant inviting all the living Nobel Peace Prize winners on an all-expenses-paid journey to Iraq. Jerusalem became Baghdad as I toured that war-torn city with two Nobel laureates. In the summer of 2000, it meant organizing the People's Campaign for Nonviolence and welcoming over five thousand people of faith to Washington, D.C., for a series of workshops, marches, and protests at the White House, the Pentagon, and the Capitol over a period of forty days.

I remember the Jesuits of El Salvador speaking to me about "the paschal mystery of Jesus" when I worked with them in 1985. At the time I did not know what they were talking about. Few people in the U.S. Church or the U.S. peace and justice movements speak about the paschal mystery. If they do, they usually mean some private piety that has nothing to do with the ongoing crucifixion of the world's poor and oppressed. But there, in El Salvador, it was the best expression the Jesuits had to explain the life-and-death struggle for justice and peace to which they would eventually give their lives. They heard the phrase from Archbishop Romero and saw how he literally shed his blood to give birth to a new El Salvador. The Jesuit martyrs taught me that struggling for faith and justice means actually, concretely, and deliberately entering into the world's bloody fray, and connecting that struggle for peace with the suffering, death, and resurrection of Jesus—who continues to suffer, die, and rise in the struggling, suffering, oppressed peoples of the world.

The Journey to Los Alamos

Recently, my Jerusalem has become Los Alamos, New Mexico, the birthplace of the bomb. Nestled in the rocky Bandelier hills, surrounded by piñon trees, cacti, and sagebrush, is the mother of all weapons of mass destruction: the Los Alamos National Laboratory. Built in 1941 by Robert Oppenheimer, the lab currently spends the largest nuclear weapons budget in history, even though the Cold War is over and the Soviet Union has collapsed. As a Christian, I have to face Los Alamos and its nuclear violence with the disruptive nonviolence of Jesus. I am called to share his paschal mystery and translate his passion into disarmament, justice, and peace here and now. Undoubtedly this gift of peace will not be well received.

Confronting Los Alamos is difficult. Few in New Mexico

criticize the lab because it is the leading moneymaker in one of the poorest states in the nation, even though the lab has contaminated our water, poisoned the land, and kept people in poverty. Indeed, it has more millionaires per capita than any other city in the United States. After the 2003 Iraq war, we pointed out how the United States sent 150,000 soldiers ten thousand miles into the Iraq desert to kill 150,000 Iraqis in an effort to find and dismantle one weapon of mass destruction, even though there were none, while still manufacturing and maintaining thousands of weapons of mass destruction right in Los Alamos. The ultimate form of terrorism, these weapons do not make us safer or more secure, we announced. Instead, they make the whole world more dangerous. They are immoral, sinful, and evil, and need to be dismantled. We call for an end to New Mexico's long, ugly nuclear history, and the creation of a New Mexico without nuclear weapons, a new land of nonviolence. Since most employees at Los Alamos are churchgoers, we also explain that Christ forbids us to support war and commands us to "love our enemies," that we cannot serve both the God of peace and the false gods of nuclear weapons.

On the morning of August 6, 2005, the sixtieth anniversary of the U.S. atomic bombing of Hiroshima and the feast of the Transfiguration, over three hundred of us gathered along the main road in town to keep vigil with our signs and banners calling for an end to that demonic work. We spoke to the media and demanded that the government spend those billions of dollars not on weapons of war but on schools, jobs, homes, health care, medicine for HIV/AIDS, environmental cleanup, and food for the starving masses. We recalled what our government had done in Japan and mourned the loss of life from these weapons. During a Eucharistic liturgy the evening before in

Santa Fe, we celebrated the transfiguration of Jesus and prayed for an end to the anti-transfiguration culture and its nuclear arsenal.

We had spent a year preparing for our action. In the course of our discernment, we decided to take up the Book of Jonah. When he called for repentance, the entire town of Nineveh put on sackcloth and ashes to repent of their violence. Inspired by the people of Nineveh, at precisely 9:00 A.M., over three hundred of us put on sackcloth, poured ashes on the ground around us, sat down in the ashes to repent of the sin of war and nuclear weapons, and prayed in silence for thirty minutes for the gift of nuclear disarmament. The ashes reminded us of the ashes of Hiroshima, as well as the actual town of Nineveh, which is known today as Mosul, in Iraq, a place reduced to ash and rubble by U.S. bombs and depleted uranium.

When we gathered afterward for our closing prayer at Ashley Pond, the place where the buildings that actually made the bomb used on Hiroshima once stood, many were in tears. None of us expected to be so moved by our action. Some said it was the greatest spiritual experience of their lives. For me, it was one of the most profound "demonstrations" I have ever attended. Perhaps the God of peace simply could not resist us and reached down and touched each one of us personally, to encourage our work for nuclear disarmament.

The use of sackcloth and ashes to repent for social sin goes back centuries. Ash Wednesday itself was built on the ancient tradition of ashes so that we might "repent and believe in the Gospel of Peace." In the Gospels of Matthew and Luke, Jesus himself affirms the act of repentance through the use of sackcloth and ashes. After the astonishing miracles he performed in the villages around Capernaum, he was upset because the people as a whole had not changed their violent ways. "Alas for you, Chorazin!" Jesus says. "Alas for you, Bethsaida! If the miracles done in your towns had been done in Tyre and Sidon, they would have repented long ago in sackcloth and ashes. Still, I tell you that it will be more bearable for Tyre and Sidon on judgment day than for you" (Matthew 11:21–22; Luke 10:13–14). If Jonah and Jesus thought Nineveh, Chorazin, and Bethsaida should have repented in sackcloth and ashes, what would they think about Los Alamos, New Mexico, where the U.S. government, and thousands of Christians, prepare to obliterate thousands of people, even destroy the entire planet, through the ongoing development of nuclear weapons?

"The atom bomb brought an empty victory to the Allied armies," Mahatma Gandhi said a few days after the atomic bombings of Hiroshima and Nagasaki. "It resulted for the time being in destroying Japan. What has happened to the soul of the destroying nation is yet too early to see." Our public witness at Los Alamos is a modest effort to reclaim our soul. We confront the nuclear weapons industry, repent of our violence, grieve the crucifixions of Hiroshima and Nagasaki, and call for the abolition of nuclear weapons and war itself because this is the spiritual journey. We cannot remain on the mountaintop, rest in the desert, or enjoy First World comforts while these weapons of mass destruction sit in our backyard. It is not a pleasant way to spend a summer day, or a happy way to practice the spiritual life, but for us, journeying to Los Alamos and disrupting the big business of nuclear weapons is the way to follow Jesus from the mountaintop to the Temple to the cross.

Jesus turned over the tables of the money changers in the Temple and gave his life with his act of civil disobedience. We believe that the global destruction planned at Los Alamos is far more sinful, idolatrous, and deadly than the injustice Jesus witnessed in the Temple. If Jesus lived in New Mexico, he would go to Los Alamos and denounce nuclear war preparations. If he lived in Washington, D.C., he would go to the Pentagon. As his followers, we have no choice but to do that work for him, to confront the institutions of war with him, and to risk the cross as he did. This is the duty of the Christian in a time of nuclear terrorism, global injustice, and massive human suffering.

Walking with Christ as He Carries His Cross

Every Christian is called to share the paschal mystery of Jesus. The Gospel invites us to join the long pilgrimage from the mystery of the Transfiguration on Mount Tabor to the paschal mystery, beginning with Jesus' civil disobedience in the Temple, the Last Supper, and his refusal to resort to violent self-defense on the Mount of Olives–and culminating in his perfect, nonviolent, suffering love on Calvary and the empty tomb. Jesus could have stayed in Galilee. He could have retreated periodically to the mountain. He could have lingered with Moses and Elijah. But he walked down the mountain, headed toward Jerusalem, entered the corrupt Temple sanctuary, broke several laws, disrupted business as usual, interfered with the banking system, and turned over the tables of the money changers. Anyone who undertook such provocative civil disobedience under that brutal empire would most assuredly have been arrested and executed. Jesus was arrested, jailed, tried, condemned, tortured, and killed–but he remained faithful and radiated perfect, nonviolent, forgiving love until his last breath. When he rose from the dead, he invited us to follow him on that same difficult road into our own paschal mystery.

If we dare undertake this discipleship journey, we have to get beyond Sunday obligations, church bingo fund-raisers, polite social behavior, inner fears, nine-to-five jobs, endless TV viewing, and American complacency to face the systemic injustice in our own backyards, wherever we live. Plans for war are developed in every single congressional district in the United States, but we can each make our own pilgrimage of Gospel nonviolence to the Pentagon; Lawrence Livermore Labs in the Bay Area; the Trident submarine bases in Florida, Connecticut, and Washington; the Strategic Air Command Base in Iowa; the Oak Ridge weapons center in Tennessee; the School of the Americas in Georgia; and the USS *Intrepid* War Museum in New York City. We have to disrupt these centers of war with the same active nonviolence Jesus used in the Temple and, like him, accept the consequences of our actions. We must expect the cross, beginning with the dismay of our relatives, the harassment of neighboring patriots, the surveillance of authorities, and perhaps even the handcuffs and jails of our own government. Not only must we expect it, but like Jesus, we must seek it.

"The Christian must have the courage to follow Christ," Thomas Merton wrote. "The Christian who is risen in Christ must dare to be like Christ. Christians must dare to follow conscience even in unpopular causes. They must if necessary be able to disagree with the majority and make decisions according to the Gospel and teachings of Christ, even when others do not understand why they are acting this way."

Christians are on a journey toward the cross. Discipleship requires conscious engagement with the forces of violence and injustice. Although we never use violence in any form, we also refuse to be passive or quiet in the face of injustice. We speak out. We take action. We turn over the tables of injustice. When we do, we take up the cross, as Jesus commanded, and share in his nonviolent, suffering love. And as we do, we know that one day we will share in an eternal transfiguration, in the new life of his resurrection.

"The most effective action we can take," Dorothy Day once said, "is to try to conform our lives to the folly of the cross." "In whatever modest and clumsy way," Daniel Berrigan writes, "we are called to honor the preference of Christ for suffering rather than inflicting suffering, for dying rather than killing." Like the saints and martyrs before us, we focus our hearts and minds on the Christ who continues to carry his cross as he transforms the world's violence and injustice into his reign of peace and justice. We join his campaign against evil and nonviolently pursue justice and peace with the same single-minded devotion, public daring, and willingness to suffer in love without retaliation. We learn from our own heroes, from Martin Luther King, Jr., Oscar Romero, the Jesuit martyr Rutilio Grande, the four martyred churchwomen of El Salvador, Rachel Corrie of Palestine, Stephen Biko of South Africa, Dorothy Stang of Brazil, and Benigno Aquino of the Philippines. Like them, we willingly offer our lives to Christ's nonviolent struggle for justice and peace, knowing that, as we do, we become part of Christ's nonviolence and will share in his victory of love, truth, and reconciliation with the entire human race.

Getting Ready for Resurrection

If we walk the way of the cross with Jesus and stay with the struggle–even if we are ignored, patronized, or mocked–we will eventually set our sights beyond the limits of the world, the struggle, and our short lifetimes, to behold Christ's reign of infinite love and perfect peace. With the transfigured light of Christ as a beacon to guide us, we will get ready for the new life of resurrection. We will start practicing resurrection. We will learn to trust that love is stronger than hate, nonviolence is stronger than violence, truth and justice are stronger than lies and injustice, and life itself is stronger than death.

The journey to the cross and the resurrection is the transfiguration journey. We realize this only at the end of the story. Matthew's Gospel concludes when the risen Jesus asks the faithful women to tell the male disciples to meet him back on the mountain in Galilee, back on Mount Tabor, the site of the Transfiguration. There they will see the risen Jesus. He is now permanently transfigured in light. He has become the Light of God, radiating throughout the earth, enlightening the human race. There on the mountain, according to Matthew, he missions the disciples to go forth and make all the nations of the world into disciples:

> The eleven disciples went to Galilee, to the mountain to
> which Jesus had ordered them. When they saw him,
> they worshiped, but they doubted. Then Jesus
> approached and said to them, "All power in heaven and
> on earth has been given to me. Go, therefore, and make
> disciples of all nations, baptizing them in the name of
> the Father, and of the Son, and of the holy Spirit,
> teaching them to observe all that I have commanded
> you. And behold, I am with you always, until the end of
> the age." (28:16–20)

On the mountain, the disciples worship and listen to the risen Jesus. He announces that all power has been given to him, that his transfiguring nonviolence is more powerful than all the weapons of the world combined, and, in effect, that the paschal mystery is God's way to disarm the planet and redeem humanity. He orders his followers to baptize not just individuals but entire nations, so that one day the whole world will practice creative nonviolence and compassionate love. Then, he promises to be with us "always."

There, at the end of the story, we realize that the Transfiguration foreshadows the new life of resurrection, and that for us, the story is just beginning. We see where we are headed—eventually to the mountain of God to dwell in God's holy peace with the risen Jesus "always." We realize that our survival is already guaranteed. We have nothing to fear. All we have to do is carry out our mission. All that is required is to accompany Jesus on the way of the cross, through our nonviolent resistance to institutionalized evil. As followers of the transfigured, risen One, we know that, even if we are harassed and persecuted, arrested and jailed, tortured and killed, we too will rise and live forever in the perfect peace of his loving presence.

From now on, we live in hope. We are no longer in the dark. For the rest of the journey, we walk in his light.

QUESTIONS FOR REFLECTION

1. How do violence, war, poverty, and nuclear weapons mock the transfigured Christ? How is the culture of violence the anti-transfiguration? What would it look like to give the transfigured Christ our complete allegiance?

2. How do you define nonviolence? How is Christ disarming you of violence? Where does Gospel nonviolence challenge you most? How can you become more loving, more nonviolent, and more compassionate?

3. How do you follow Christ down the mountain? What is the Jerusalem that you are headed toward? How do you oppose injustice, greed, war, nuclear weapons, and the culture of violence?

4. What does the cross mean for you? How do you practice

creative nonviolence and resist systemic injustice? What keeps you from carrying on Christ's mission of nonviolent, suffering love in resistance to systemic injustice?

5. Where do you need to be healed? How do you heal others? How can you spend more time in prayer and fasting so that your life brings greater healing and peace to others? How do you expel the demons of violence and death from those around you and from the culture of war?

6. What does it mean for you to share in the paschal mystery of Christ? How can you accompany Christ as he goes to the cross and the resurrection, and share in his work to disarm, transform, and heal humanity?

7. Where do you find hope? What hopeful deeds can you engage in to help bring hope to others?

———

Dear Jesus,

Help me to go down the mountain with you and accompany you on the way of the cross, that I too might confront and resist systemic injustice with your loving nonviolence, that I too might accept suffering with love and forgiveness and not a trace of revenge or retaliation in the struggle for justice, that I too might enter the new life of resurrection.

Help me to pray and fast, that I might expel the demons of war and death from others and heal others to live in the Holy Spirit of love and life.

Heal me that I might always walk beside you on the path of love, nonviolence, and peace.

Make me your faithful disciple and friend to transform our anti-transfiguration world of war, violence, and nuclear weapons, that we might all welcome your reign of peace and love. Amen.

PART FIVE

THE MISSION OF TRANSFIGURATION NONVIOLENCE

Steps Along the Transfiguration Journey

1. Ponder where the light of the transfigured Christ is shining, and step into the light.

2. Reflect on the mission that God has given you with your life, and how you are fulfilling it.

3. Commit yourself once again to fulfilling the mission of love, compassion, and peace that Christ has given you.

4. Ponder the fullest, best life that you can offer Christ after your death, and set yourself to living that life of loving service.

5. Join the nonviolent movements for justice, disarmament,

and peace, and work publicly for the abolition of war, poverty, injustice, environmental destruction, and nuclear weapons.

6. See your life journey as contributing to the transfiguration, the disarmament and nonviolent transformation of humanity.

7. Help others fulfill their mission of transfiguration nonviolence.

8. Get ready for eternity by living every moment from now on as if you are already in heaven. Go deeper into the peace of the present moment, embody nonviolence, become the light, allow God to shine through you, radiate universal love and infinite compassion, so that your very presence is disarming, healing, and enlightening.

9. With every step, walk and breathe in the Holy Spirit of peace. Let peace dwell within you, above you, underneath you, and around you. Make peace with yourself, your family and friends, and the whole human race.

_____

19

Transfiguration Today

M artin Luther King, Jr., never spoke about his own spiritual life, private prayer, or personal relationship with God, except for one astonishing event.

It was the beginning of the Montgomery bus boycott. Rosa Parks had been arrested on December 1, 1955, for refusing to relinquish her bus seat to a white man. Overnight, Dr. King was catapulted into the leadership of the new movement and suddenly developed a bold voice denouncing the evils of racism, violence, and injustice. Privately, however, King was a reluctant prophet. He did not seek the spotlight or understand the principles of nonviolence, much less the long-term implications of this campaign of resistance. Few could have foreseen the upheaval he would lead.

Like the other organizers, King originally thought the boycott would last only a few days. But as days turned into weeks and months, white Montgomery redoubled their hostile efforts to maintain segregation. Klansmen threatened the Baptist ministers who led the movement. Dr. King began to receive calls ordering him to stop the boycott or be killed. Two months into the boycott, King was arrested and jailed on a false charge of speeding. For a few hours, he thought he might be driven out to the boondocks and lynched. Because of the public outcry and media interest, he was released. But after that, he received up to a dozen death threats a day. At times, he was overwhelmed by fear, and, for a while, the hero of nonviolence slept with a gun underneath his pillow and armed guards watching his house.

As David Garrow explains in the biography *Bearing the Cross*, King's struggle of faith reached a crescendo on Friday night, January 27, 1956. That night, after a long, exhausting strategy session, King returned home at midnight. His wife, Coretta, and their new baby girl were sound asleep.

But King was preoccupied, worried, and too scared to sleep. Then the phone rang, and a sneering, sinister voice told him that he must leave Montgomery immediately or he would be killed within a few days. After a flurry of foul language, the caller hung up. King was devastated. This was the last straw. He could not take it anymore. Frightened and at his wit's end, he went to make himself a cup of coffee and sat alone at his kitchen table. Putting his head down, he started to pray.

For the rest of his life, King would look back on the moment that followed as the most profound spiritual experience of his life. For the first time, he realized God was personal because, out of the blue, just at that second, he had a personal experience of God. This transfiguration moment gave him the strength to carry on the struggle, lead the movement, and face his cross. It was the only experience of God that he spoke about in all his talks and lectures around the country. He wrote about it in his first book, *Stride Toward Freedom*:

> I was ready to give up. With my cup of coffee sitting untouched before me, I tried to think of a way to move out of the picture without appearing a coward. In this state of exhaustion, when my courage had all but gone, I decided to take my problem to God. With my head in my hands, I bowed over the kitchen table and prayed aloud.
>
> The words I spoke to God that midnight are still vivid in my memory. "I am here taking a stand for what I believe is right. But now I am afraid. The people are looking to me for leadership, and if I stand before them without strength and courage, they too will falter. I am at the end of my powers. I have nothing left. I've come to the point where I can't face it alone."
>
> At that moment, I experienced the presence of the Divine as I had never experienced God before. It seemed as though I could hear the quiet assurance of an inner voice saying: "Stand up for justice, stand up for truth, and God will be at your side forever." Almost at once my fears began to go. My uncertainty disappeared. I was ready to face anything. (King, *Stride Toward Freedom* [New York: Harper and Row, 1958], 114–15)

Three days later, King's house was bombed and his family nearly killed. "Strangely enough, I accepted the word of the bombing calmly," King wrote. "My religious experience a few nights before had given me the strength to face it."

When angry crowds gathered in front of his house an hour

after the bombing, King emerged and addressed them from the ruins of his front porch. In the heat of the moment, when the angry mob was ready to riot on white Montgomery, King gave a spontaneous talk about nonviolence and the command to love one's enemies. Not only was it one of the most inspiring talks he ever gave but it literally disarmed the crowd and saved the lives of several white police officers. "We must meet hate with love," King said that night. "If I am stopped, this movement will not stop because God is with the movement. Go home with this glorious faith and this radiant assurance." As King reflected later, "A night that seemed destined to end in unleashed chaos came to a close in a majestic group demonstration of nonviolence." Those inspiring words that transformed the crowd and reenergized their commitment to nonviolence occurred because of the affirming words King had heard during his transfiguration moment a few days earlier.

Up until that midnight encounter with God at his kitchen table, King had never before felt the presence of God, he said eleven years later in a public address. "I had never felt an experience with God. It seemed at that moment, I could hear an inner voice saying to me, 'Martin Luther, stand up for righteousness. Stand up for justice. Stand up for truth. And lo, I will be with you, even until the end of the world.' I heard the voice of Jesus saying to fight on. He promised never to leave me, never to leave me alone."

Exactly one year after that momentous midnight experience, King awoke to find twelve sticks of dynamite on his front porch with the fuse still smoldering. That morning, he preached again about his religious experience one year earlier, and thanked God for the strength he had been given to carry on the struggle for justice, even in the face of certain assassination. "You gave me a vision in the kitchen of my house," King prayed out loud, "and I am thankful for it. So I am not afraid of anybody this morning. Tell Montgomery they can keep shooting and I'm going to stand up to them. Tell Montgomery they can keep bombing and I'm going to stand up to them. If I had to die tomorrow morning, I would die happy because I've been to the mountaintop and I've seen the promised land and it's going to be here in Montgomery."

King never forgot that midnight experience. He was able to maintain his strength, faith, and steadfast nonviolence throughout the next twelve years because of that personal encounter with God and the transfiguring words of affirmation he heard. On April 3, 1968, the night before he was assassinated in Memphis, King repeated that claim. He announced again that he had been to the mountaintop, had looked over, and had seen the promised land. He knew that he might not make it to the promised land, but he knew that those who struggle for justice and peace would. He was filled with hope because of that one spiritual experience at his kitchen table. God had spoken to Martin Luther King and strengthened him, so he in turn was able to speak to the rest of us and help us continue the journey of Gospel nonviolence to the cross.

At some point, all the saints and martyrs of history experienced a transfiguration moment. As they undertook the risky journey of the Gospel, and followed Jesus to the cross, they must have heard words of consolation, affirmation, and encouragement, as Jesus did on Mount Tabor. They too must have felt the glory of God shine through them. They too must have radiated the light of God and dispelled the darkness around them.

They too must have been disarmed and sent forth on the journey of transfiguring nonviolence. From the martyrs of the early Church through the desert fathers and mothers, the brilliant example of Francis and Clare, and the daring engagement of Ignatius and the early Jesuits to the great figures of the last century, such as Franz Jägerstätter, Dorothy Day, Mohandas Gandhi, Mother Teresa, and Oscar Romero, God has consistently encouraged those who followed the transfigured Jesus and given them a transfiguration moment.

Another astonishing example of transfiguration occurs in the last days of Thomas Merton. For twenty-seven years, Merton had spent seven hours a day in formal prayer at the Trappist monastery of Gethsemani in Kentucky. Through his voluminous writings, he had spoken out against nuclear war, racism, injustice, and the Vietnam War long before any other U.S. priest or major religious leader did. When a new, open-minded abbot was elected in early 1968, Merton was allowed to accept an invitation to the East, where he led retreats, met the Dalai Lama, and studied Buddhism. After giving a lecture to a worldwide gathering of monks in Bangkok, on December 10, 1968, he retired to his room for an afternoon nap; he was accidentally electrocuted by a faulty fan.

Years later, when his diary *The Asian Journal* was published, readers discovered that Merton had undergone the most profound personal spiritual experience of his long spiritual journey while viewing the huge Buddhist statues near the remote village of Polonnaruwa, in present-day Sri Lanka. It occurred just a few days before his death.

I am able to approach the Buddhas barefoot and undisturbed, my feet in wet grass, wet sand. Then the

silence of the extraordinary faces. The great smiles. Huge
and yet subtle. Filled with every possibility, questioning
nothing, knowing everything, rejecting nothing, the
peace not of emotional resignation but of Madhyamika,
of sunyata, that has seen through every question without
trying to discredit anyone or anything–without
refutation–without establishing some other argument.
For the doctrinaire, the mind that needs well-established
positions, such peace, such silence, can be frightening. I
was knocked over with a rush of relief and thankfulness
at the obvious clarity of the figures, the clarity and
fluidity of shape and line, the design of the monumental
bodies composed into the rock shape and landscape.
Looking at these figures I was suddenly, almost forcibly,
jerked clean out of the habitual, half-tied vision of things,
and an inner clearness, clarity, as if exploding from the
rocks themselves, became evident and obvious. The
thing about all this is that there is no puzzle, no
problem, and really no "mystery." All problems are
resolved and everything is clear, simply because what
matters is clear. The rock, all matter, all life, is charged
with dharmakaya. Everything is emptiness and
everything is compassion. I don't know when in my life
I have ever had such a sense of beauty and spiritual
validity running together in one aesthetic illumination.
Surely my Asian pilgrimage has come clear and purified
itself. I mean, I know and have seen what I was
obscurely looking for. I don't know what else remains
but I have now seen and have pierced through the
surface and have got beyond the shadow and the
disguise. This is Asia in its purity. It is clear, pure,

complete. It says everything; it needs nothing. And because it needs nothing it can afford to be silent, unnoticed, undiscovered. It does not need to be discovered. It is we, Asians included, who need to discover it. (Merton, *The Asian Journal* [New York: New Directions, 1973], 233–37)

Merton's life was a long spiritual pilgrimage, and at the end, he experienced God in this moment of "illumination." His transfiguration experience confirmed his life search. He became like the transfigured Christ, shared in Christ's cross and resurrection, and continues to shed light for thousands of people around the world.

When Did We Experience Transfiguration?

In the sayings of the desert fathers and mothers, the story is told about Abba Lot, who went to Abba Joseph for advice. "As much as I can, I practice a spiritual discipline," he said. "I keep the fasts. I say my prayers. I take time for meditation, and I keep quiet. As much as possible I keep my thoughts clean. What else should I do?"

The old monk stood up and stretched out his hands toward heaven, and his fingers became like torches of flames. Then he said, "Why not be turned into fire?"

If we dare follow Jesus on the way to the cross, at some point we too will be transfigured. Like King and Merton and the desert fathers and mothers, we will feel the light and glory of God moving through us in a spiritual "illumination" that will empower us to carry on the journey of nonviolent resistance to injustice and to radiate the presence of God around us. Our transfiguration moment may come through prayer, listening to Christ, seeking God, and struggling against imperial injustice and institutionalized violence, but ultimately it is not something we earn or deserve. It is a gift we receive with gratitude so that we can continue the Gospel journey to the cross. In this transfiguration moment, we are filled with the Holy Spirit of God. Like Jesus, we glimpse the new life of resurrection to come. We are filled with divine light to see the path ahead more clearly, and we feel encouraged to complete the journey, as Jesus and Dr. King did. This enlightenment will shed new light on the meaning and purpose of our lives, as Merton confessed, and we will be able to go forward on the journey with "clarity."

The saints knew from firsthand experience that if we follow Jesus from his baptism through his public ministry to his cross and resurrection, practice his teachings, and perform his works of mercy, healing, and peace, at some point we too will share his transfiguration. The saints demonstrate that we too can radiate divine light, grace, and truth. We too can experience being the beloved children of God. We too can become channels of God's light and glory to a dark and broken world. But this transfiguration moment is not cheap or easy. It does not necessarily "feel good." It comes to those who sacrifice themselves through pain, hard work, risk taking, compassionate love, selfless service, and nonviolent struggle on behalf of suffering humanity. It is God's way of affirming that struggle.

According to the Acts of the Apostles, the early Christian community experienced the light of transfiguration in the upper room behind locked doors when the Holy Spirit came upon them as tongues of fire. Each of them radiated the light of Christ, and they were transformed. They immediately took to the streets, announced the good news of the nonviolent Christ, and denounced the war-making empire–and they did this for the rest of their lives, until their own inevitable martyrdoms.

"At some moments, we experience complete unity within us and around us," Henri Nouwen wrote. "This is the experience that Peter, James and John had on the top of Mount Tabor when they saw the aspect of Jesus' face change and his clothing become sparkling white. They wanted that moment to last forever. This is the experience of the fullness of time. These moments are given to us so that we can remember them when God seems far away and everything appears empty and useless. These experiences are true moments of grace."

If we undertake a prayerful review of our lives, we may recall a moment when we felt the presence of God, when we heard divine words of encouragement, when we radiated the transfiguring light of Christ, or when we realized the glory of God shining through us. The point is not necessarily to seek such moments or to cling to those peak experiences, as the disciples wanted to do on Mount Tabor. Rather, first and foremost, we are to seek God and do God's will, to follow Jesus, and to challenge the principalities and powers that crucify Christ again today in the world's poor. Transfiguration moments are meant to affirm the journey of nonviolent resistance. These enlightenment experiences are God's way of supporting and consoling those who seek justice, make peace, heal the broken, liberate the oppressed, beat swords into plowshares, and reconcile humanity.

Getting Ready for Transfiguration

To radiate the light of Christ and share his Transfiguration, we have to become mature Christians. Christ does not want us to remain infants in the spiritual life, to rely on spiritual baby food. Rather, he wants us to grow up, to become wiser, to be "learned in the kingdom," to be born again, to become children of the light who live in the reign of God. Christ seeks serious, faithful disciples who will share his paschal mystery and carry on the torch of nonviolent love and peace.

Wholehearted discipleship to Jesus is the greatest work we can undertake. To be his mature followers, we have to undergo the turmoil of King, Merton, and the saints, and seek God with all our hearts and minds. We too must speak out against injustice, practice creative nonviolence, engage in contemplative prayer, love everyone we meet, and take greater risks for the truth of disarmament and social justice. As we do, we will receive affirmation and encouragement, and gladly walk all the way to our own experience of the cross and resurrection.

That means that we have to get ready for transfiguration. Like King and Merton, we have to take a stand, be faithful to God, say our prayers, speak the truth, love everyone, practice nonviolence, and be open to the action of God in our hearts and lives. We too have to put our heads down on the kitchen table sometimes and turn to God in prayer. We too have to undertake a spiritual pilgrimage and open our minds and hearts to the new movements of the Holy Spirit of peace. We too have to be ready for God when God decides to touch us and speak to us.

As we walk the discipleship journey toward transfiguration and the paschal mystery, we try to live in the present moment. We try to be completely aware of ourselves so that we are fully present to others, so that we become transparent to others and the light of the transfigured Christ can shine through us. As the Buddhists suggest, we practice mindfulness and attend even to our breath so that we remain centered, calm, at peace, ready for Christ. No matter where we are, no matter what is happening to us, no matter what pain or suffering we endure, we can still center ourselves in the present moment and prepare for enlightenment, that Christ might shine through us, that we might radiate his love and peace to the world, that we too might taste the new life of resurrection to come.

As more and more of us enter into the light, grace, and peace of the present moment, fully aware and alive to the Holy Spirit within and among us, we become communal instruments of social transformation that can transfigure not only our own lives but even the world.

Global Transfiguration

Just as we each might personally experience a transfiguration moment when the light of Christ shines through us, entire communities and nations can experience a social transfiguration where the light of Christ leads the movement of nonviolent resistance toward a breakthrough of truth, justice, disarmament, and peace. Throughout history, there have been many social transfigurations. The abolitionist movement, the suffragist movement, the civil rights movement, and the Plowshares disarmament movement were remarkable, historic transfiguration moments that led to greater justice and peace. The fall of the Berlin Wall, the People Power movement of the Philippines, and the nonviolent resistance movement in Lithuania are other recent examples.

One of the brightest transfiguration moments the world has recently seen occurred in South Africa, as decades of apartheid ended with the release of Nelson Mandela from prison, his election as president, the creation of a new, democratic South Africa, and the work of the Truth and Reconciliation Commission led by the Nobel Peace Prize winner Archbishop Desmond Tutu. After years of racial hatred and oppression, South Africa seemed destined to self-destruction and civil war, but instead, the suffering love and wisdom of its leaders brought healing, racial justice, and democracy. So great was the social transfiguration of South Africa that Mandela even ordered the abolition of the death penalty and the dismantling of their six nuclear weapons in an act of unilateral, national nuclear disarmament. Tutu later wrote that the first free election in South Africa was a transfiguration moment for the whole country that shone brightly around the whole world. In recent years, as South Africans struggled against poverty and HIV/AIDS, he wrote that transfiguration is "an ongoing process," a journey toward other new transfigurations.

Northern Ireland experienced a similar transfiguration moment. After thirty years of British occupation, the civil war of the "Troubles," the deaths of fifteen hundred people, and the imprisonment of thousands more, the Irish Republican Army announced a cease-fire and began secret negotiations with the British toward a political settlement. The breakthrough occurred on Good Friday 1998. While living in Derry, Northern Ireland, that year, I witnessed the light that shone through the Good Friday peace agreement. For a brief time, everyone experienced a moment of hope and felt encouraged by the real possibility that the never-ending war might actually end and a new day of peace and resurrection might dawn. The journey toward peace and freedom continues, but their uphill struggle may have indeed ended with that peak experience.

Still another example occurred in the months after the

September 11, 2001, attacks, when many felt despair not only because of the horrific terrorism but because of the U.S. retaliatory response in the bombing of Afghanistan and Iraq. During those initial dark months, some family members who lost loved ones in the 9/11 attacks joined together to speak out against war and urge peaceful resolutions. In a sense, they were transfigured and formed September Eleventh Families for Peaceful Tomorrows, a nonprofit, antiwar group in memory of their deceased loved ones. Their first public action was a 250-mile walk from New York's Ground Zero to the ruins of the Pentagon. Then they sent a delegation to Afghanistan to listen to the Afghani families who lost loved ones during the U.S. bombing raids. Instead of giving in to despair and discouragement, they became signs of light and hope and encouraged others to confront U.S. retaliatory war-making, to end our own terrorist attacks, and to create a more nonviolent world.

If we look closely, we can see signs of God's light breaking through our darkness and despair, giving us hope and encouragement, sending us forth to complete the work of justice and disarmament. One day, when the people of the United States finally wake up; dismantle their nuclear weapons; spend their billions of dollars to eradicate hunger, disease, homelessness, illiteracy, and unemployment; clean up the oceans and the earth; and renounce war forever, humanity itself will be transfigured and the light of Christ will shine brightly and lead us to an astonishing breakthrough of global hope and encouragement. Humanity will catch a glimpse of the nonviolent reign of God and set to work preparing to welcome its full arrival.

These transfiguration moments, whether individual or collective or even, one day, global, urge us to complete the mission Christ has given us. Like Martin Luther King, Jr., Thomas Merton, and the saints, each one of us has been sent into the world of violence on the mission of transfiguration nonviolence. That is the task left for us.

20.

Fulfilling Our Mission

When Jesus was transfigured on Mount Tabor, Moses and Elijah encouraged him to fulfill his mission, his "exodus," which would liberate humanity from its slavery to violence and death. Jesus faced the most daunting mission of all: to practice perfect nonviolence, confront imperial injustice, denounce corrupt religion, reach out with all-inclusive love, suffer torture and death without a trace of anger or retaliation, and until his last cry, demonstrate forgiveness, faithfulness, and hope.

Jesus fulfilled his mission perfectly. By all accounts, he was the embodiment of love, the incarnation of divine nonviolence. After his resurrection, he called his disciples to carry on that mission, to join God's work of disarming love, and to spend every minute until their dying breath to complete that mission.

God has a mission for each one of us. God needs each one

of us to do some specific work during our short time on earth. Only we can do the work that God requires of us. Each one of us needs to fulfill this mission of love and peace that God intends for us. Accomplishing our mission of love and peace is actually the most fulfilling work we can do because it is the completion of our spiritual journey, our destiny.

Because we are transfiguration people, our job is to complete our mission. As we pursue God and God's reign through faithful discipleship to the nonviolent Jesus, we will learn what our divine mission is. The closer we come to reaching those heights of love, the more we too will meet saints and prophets who will confirm our mission and encourage us to complete it. Perhaps God will even speak to us directly with words of consolation, confirmation, and affirmation.

"We are called by Jesus to transfigure the world we live in and to bring the glory of God to the places and situations that are most in need of glory, hope and the presence of God," the theologian Megan McKenna writes. In a world of disfiguring violence, I think our mission is to do the work of transfiguring nonviolence. This mission pushes us into the world of war, injustice, and nuclear weapons to teach nonviolence, proclaim nonviolence, practice nonviolence, and prepare our world of violence to be transformed by God into a new realm of loving nonviolence.

Thomas Merton explained this mission in a powerful essay published by *The Catholic Worker* in September 1961. "Truly we have entered the 'post-Christian era' with a vengeance," he wrote. "Whether we are destroyed or whether we survive, the future is awful to contemplate." Then he asked, "What are we to do?" With unusual bluntness, he answered his own question:

The duty of the Christian in this time of crisis is to strive with all their power and intelligence, with their faith, their hope in Christ, and love for God and humanity, to do the one task which God has imposed upon us in the world today. That task is to work for the total abolition of war. There can be no question that unless war is abolished the world will remain constantly in a state of madness and desperation in which, because of the immense destructive power of modern weapons, the danger of catastrophe will be imminent and probable at every moment everywhere. Unless we set ourselves immediately to this task, both as individuals and in our political and religious groups, we tend by our very passivity and fatalism to cooperate with the destructive forces that are leading inexorably to war. It is a problem of terrifying complexity and magnitude, for which the church itself is not fully able to see clear and decisive solutions. Yet she must lead the way on the road to the nonviolent settlement of difficulties and toward the gradual abolition of war as the way of settling international or civil disputes. Christians must become active in every possible way, mobilizing all their resources for the fight against war. We may never succeed in this campaign, but whether we succeed or not, the duty is evident. (In James Forest, *Living with Wisdom* [New York: Orbis Books, 1991], 137–38)

Merton sums up the Christian mission as the task of disarmament. We are to disarm one another and disarm our world. We are to make war obsolete. From now on, anyone who claims to be a follower of the nonviolent Jesus in a world of violence must renounce violence, speak out against war, pray for the end of war, oppose our government's preparations for war, dismantle the weapons of war, disrupt the culture of war, and create a spiritual community that radiates the opposite of war, an all-encompassing love that breeds true peace for the entire human race. This is an impossible task, yet it is precisely the mission imposed upon us by God. Each one of us is required to contribute to the disarmament and nonviolent transformation of the world, to help one another toward transfiguration.

To enter the transfiguration story, follow the nonviolent Jesus, and fulfill our mission of disarming love, we need to discern the movement of the Holy Spirit among us so that we are led by God and actually doing the job God wants of us. Certainly this discernment requires contemplative meditation, quiet listening, and intercessory prayer. But it also needs the help of other peacemaking Christians. We cannot fulfill our mission alone. We need the help of a local peace and justice group who engage in a public stand against injustice and war and for justice and peace. With other like-minded peacemakers, we will take to the streets, announce the good news of peace, and disarm the culture. We will carry on the transfiguration journey all the way to the cross and resurrection and into the streets, and we will engage in our own modern-day acts of the apostles. Like the early community, we will be transformed into a dynamic, creative, public force for love and peace that witnesses to Christ and fulfills the mission of transfiguration nonviolence.

Along the way, we will be confirmed in our mission. We will resolve to remain faithful to the task of disarmament. We will find the strength to walk forward into the world and die well with that same radiant love, truth, and peace. We will play our part in the transfiguration, the disarmament of the world.

As transfiguration people, we embody nonviolence, breathe in peace, breathe out peace, walk gently upon the earth, love everyone with kindness and compassion, and serve those in need. We are fully alive, fully alert, fully aware of ourselves and reality, trying to live in the present moment. Life becomes one long, glorious transfiguration. We are born again, risen, already in heaven, even as we head toward heaven and the new life of resurrection. Eternal life, we realize, has begun—right now, this minute. The reign of God has arrived.

Each one of us is summoned to fulfill this great mission. God is leading us on our journey through life to accomplish God's work of compassionate love and disarming peace. When we finally meet God face-to-face, we will understand the mission that had been given to us, and realize that we were never alone, that we had nothing to fear, and that all we had to do was be faithful to the discipleship journey and the work of transfiguration nonviolence.

With the grace of that knowledge and awareness, we step into the light and live out our holy mission of transfiguration nonviolence, so that our story might be part of his story and, one day, his mission might be complete in us.

QUESTIONS FOR REFLECTION

1. At what point in your life were you transfigured like Christ? When have you felt enlightened by Christ? How does the light of Christ shine through you?

2. Where do you see the light of Christ shining in and through communities around the world today, in the nonviolent movements of social transfiguration?

3. What is the mission that Christ has given you? What do you need to do to fulfill that mission so that, by the time of your death, you will have accomplished your mission for Christ?

4. How can you connect your life more and more to the mission of Jesus, so that you too live a life of unconditional love,

boundless compassion, creative nonviolence, steadfast resistance to evil, and perfect peace toward everyone?

5. How do you contribute to the transfiguration, the nonviolent transformation, of the whole human race?

6. How can you become a better teacher, practitioner, and apostle of transfiguration nonviolence?

7. What would it look like and how would it feel to live fully alive in the present moment right now, fully aware and conscious of reality? How can you live more fully and aware of each moment so that every moment is a transfiguration moment, so that you walk in the light of Christ, so that you already live in the peaceful reign of God?

———————

Dear Jesus,

Please help me to fulfill my mission on earth, that I might join you in your mission of transfiguration nonviolence, that I might accompany you in your work to disarm, transform, heal, and redeem humanity.

Make me an instrument of your love and peace.

Disarm my heart and send me forth into the world of war and violence that I might disarm others and welcome your reign of peace and nonviolence.

Help me to live each moment in peace.

Help me never to hurt another person again.

Give me the grace to resist and transform the structures of

violence, to help build a global grassroots movement of transfiguration nonviolence, so that one day we might abolish war, injustice, poverty, and nuclear weapons, and everyone might live in the light of your transfiguration peace. Amen.

CONCLUSION

The story of the transfiguration of Jesus outlines the discipleship journey, the journey of life itself. Jesus climbs the mountain of God to pray about his upcoming journey. He is transformed into the Light of God and encouraged by the saints and prophets to fulfill his mission. Finally, he heads down the mountain to Jerusalem, where he confronts imperial injustice, suffers death on the cross, enters the new life of resurrection, and returns to invite us to undertake that same salvific, spiritual journey of Gospel nonviolence.

The spiritual life can be summed up as the journey through life in the footsteps of Jesus on the road to peace. At some point, we too climb a holy mountain to pray to God. At some point, we wake up and recognize the presence of Christ in our midst— in the faces of one another, the poor, the oppressed, the outsider, and the enemy. At some point, we feel enlightened by Christ. At some point, we hear the affirmation of the saints and prophets around us, encouraging us to complete our Gospel mission of love, truth, and compassion. We realize that God wants us to listen to Jesus and follow him faithfully on the journey of love through life. At some point, we too walk down the mountain into the broken world toward our own modern-day Jerusalems, to confront systemic injustice with active nonviolence in pursuit of disarmament and justice. Like Jesus, we take up our cross of creative nonviolence, resistance to evil, and redemptive, suffering love. In that suffering, dying love, we experience resurrection. Our journey then will be complete.

Transfiguration leads us into the paschal mystery of Jesus. As his disciples, we share in his cross and resurrection. We know the slight edge of life over death. We radiate the light of truth in a world of darkness and lies. We walk with faith, hope, and love, despite the idolatry, despair, and fear around us. We offer compassion and mercy in a cruel, merciless world. We forgive and love, even though such forgiveness and love is outdated, even outlawed. We believe in God, and so we resist evil and suffer the consequences of our nonviolent resistance. We obey the law of God, and so we civilly disobey the unjust laws that legalize hunger, injustice, and nuclear weapons. We stand for peace, even as others wave the flag of war and march off to massacre the poor in the latest slaughter.

We have seen Christ on our own mountaintop, transfiguration moments, and so we are witnesses of the transfigured Christ. We have been enlightened by the light of Christ and have woken up to the present moment. We live and breathe in peace, listen to Jesus, love and forgive everyone, and spread healing light and love through our very presence. We walk on, like the transfigured, risen Christ, into the anti-transfiguration world of disfiguring violence on the Gospel mission of transfiguring nonviolence to disarm and heal others, and to help one another enter the light of Christ, until the whole human race is enlightened and the whole world is transfigured into God's reign of love and peace.

From now on, we are transfiguration people.

ABOUT THE AUTHOR

John Dear is a priest, pastor, and peacemaker. An internationally recognized voice for peace, he has served as the director of the Fellowship of Reconciliation, an interfaith peace organization; a Red Cross coordinator of chaplains in New York City after the September 11, 2001, attacks; and the pastor of several churches. He lives in the desert of northern New Mexico and speaks each year in churches and universities to tens of thousands of people. For information, see www.johndear.org.